Order by Accident

Order by Accident

The Origins and Consequences of Conformity in Contemporary Japan

Alan S. Miller
Satoshi Kanazawa

Westview
PRESS
A Member of the Perseus Books Group

Copyright © 2000 by Westview Press, A Member of the Perseus Books Group

Published in 2000 in the United States of America by Westview Press, 5500 Central Avenue, Boulder, Colorado 80301-2877, and in the United Kingdom by Westview Press, 12 Hid's Copse Road, Cumnor Hill, Oxford OX2 9JJ

Find us on the World Wide Web at www.westviewpress.com

Library of Congress Cataloging-in-Publication Data

A CIP catalog record for this book is available from the Library of Congress.
ISBN 0-8133-3921-9

The paper used in this publication meets the requirements of the American National Standard for Permanence of Paper for Printed Library Materials Z39.48-1984.

PERSEUS
POD
ON DEMAND

10   9   8   7   6   5   4   3   2   1

This book is dedicated to my parents, Joseph and Thelma Miller, who never discouraged me from pursuing my interests, even though, in retrospect, they often should have.—A.S.M.

To Michael Hechter, without whom I would not be interested in Japan in the slightest.—S.K.

Contents

Tables and Figures

Figures

Acknowledgments

A number of people helped with this book, either by providing useful comments and suggestions, or merely by providing us with the intellectual tools necessary to undertake such a project. Alphabetically, they are: Herbert Costner, Michael Hechter, Miyoko Hiramine, Christine Horne, Tatsuya Kameda, Atsushi Naoi, Fred Nick, Fumiaki Ojima, Elliott Sober, Rodney Stark, Yoriko Watanabe, David Sloan Wilson, Toshio Yamagishi, and Masaki Yuki. Special thanks to the graduate students in the department of behavioral sciences at Hokkaido University for gathering information, and to the Institute of Statistical Mathematics for providing data. Also, we thank Takashi Yoshiwa and the people at Recruit Corporation's Sapporo Branch for permission to take the photograph used on the cover. Finally, the support of the people at Westview, especially Andrew Day, made the process of publishing this manuscript easy and enjoyable.

Alan S. Miller
Satoshi Kanazawa

PART ONE

Theoretical Orientation

1

Social Order and Social Control: An Introduction

For many Westerners, Japanese society has often provided an interesting area of study. Although Japan is a modern industrialized country, in many ways it differs dramatically from Western, and even other Eastern, modern industrialized societies. Japan's differences from Western societies are especially evident when comparing Japan with the United States. Both Japan and the United States are technologically advanced and highly urban countries with democratic political systems and capitalist economies. They are also the two leading world economic powers, as well as strong military allies. But they are also fundamentally different. The differences are not merely cultural by-products, based on differences in race, language, and religion. The differences are specifically related to the structures of each society—to the relationships among people and between people and social institutions, and as such, represent an explicit desire to organize their societies differently.

This book explores how social order is produced and maintained in Japan. By social order we mean the degree to which people follow explicit and implicit rules of behavior. That is, a society where the great majority of citizens obey laws and conform to social norms can be described as having a high degree of social order. Japan is such a society. This books seeks to explain why social order is high in Japan (and, by implication, why it is relatively low in many other countries, particularly in the United States). However, rather than relying on ill-defined concepts of culture or tradition, the focus is primarily on understanding specific social psychological processes that occur in small groups, and how these social control mechanisms produce both desirable and undesirable consequences at higher levels of social aggregation. In doing so, this book attempts to integrate a wide range of scholarship on Japan, ranging from studies by criminologists to religious studies to the most current social psychological studies.

Ironies of Social Structure

The way a society is organized, both in terms of the characteristics of its institutions and the interaction patterns that emerge at the small-group level, has profound effects that are often unintentional and nonintuitive. Consider Tables 1.1 and 1.2. They list the number of Nobel Prizes won by various countries and the homicide rate of various countries, respectively.

As can be seen, the United States has produced more Nobel Prize winners than any other country. (This is true even when we remove scholars who were born in other countries.) The United States also has the highest homicide rate of any modern industrialized country. Conversely, Japan has produced very few Nobel Prize winners, despite having a technologically advanced society and highly educated citizenry. It also has the lowest homicide rate of any modern industrialized country. These facts are not unrelated. Rather, they are related to fundamental differences in how the societies are organized and how social order is produced and maintained. This book explores those differences. People interested in understanding why Japanese society runs so smoothly with as little crime and social problems as it does will find the answer here. However, these answers do not necessarily translate into "lessons" for other countries, particularly for the United States. Safety and security comes with a price, a price that people in other countries might find too high. Of course, societies that are low in social order, such as American society, have their own price tag, a price many Japanese would not be willing to pay. There are no simple answers.

This introduction likely strikes the reader as overly pessimistic. One can surely lower the crime rate in the United States without paying too high a price. Of course this is possible. Other countries that are far more similar to the United States than Japan is, such as Canada, have relatively low crime rates. But there is something unique about American society that makes the task daunting, just as there is something unique about Japanese society that makes the task relatively easy. That is also what this book is about.

Safety is a two-edged sword: The line between "order" and "obedience" is very thin. Freedom is also a two-edged sword: The line between "liberty" and "anarchy" is also very thin. At issue are the concepts of social order and social control. What type of order do people want in their society, and what means of control are acceptable?

Although the main task of this book is to present a general theory of social order and then use it to explain how order is maintained in modern Japanese society, it is also meant as a comparative work. By highlighting how social order is maintained in Japan, one can also gain some insight into why Japanese society differs significantly from many other

TABLE 1.1   Total Number of Nobel Prizes Won (Through 1995)

Country	Awards
United States	180
U.K.	67
Germany	61
France	25
Sweden	15
Switzerland	13
Former USSR	10
Netherlands	10
Austria	9
Denmark	8
Italy	7
Canada	7
Belgium	5
Japan	5

SOURCE: Japan Science and Technology Agency (1997).

TABLE 1.2   Homicide Rate per 100,000 Population

Country	Rate
United States	9.0
Italy	5.3
Denmark	5.1
Australia	4.9
Germany	3.9
Austria	3.5
Belgium	3.4
Switzerland	3.1
Scotland	2.2
Canada	2.0
U.K.	1.4
Japan	1.4

SOURCE: United Nations World Crime Survey (1995).

societies. The difficulty will be in determining whether those differences are for the best.

Social Order

For the purpose of this book, we will use a very simple definition of social order. Following Kanazawa (1997) we propose that social order exists to the degree that people in a society follow the rules. By rules, we mean both explicit rules (i.e., laws) and implicit rules of appropriate conduct (i.e., norms and mores). Thus, order is a continuum. It exists to some extent in all societies, even those undergoing turbulent revolutions, since it is always the case that most people will still follow the basic rules of society. However, order exists at differing levels. It is relatively easy to compare societies in terms of explicit rule following since we can compare crime rates cross-nationally. (Actually, this is a rather difficult task because of different definitions of crimes, reporting of crimes, and ability of the police to enforce crimes in each society.) However, even if one is able to construct comparable crime data and compare the data across societies, only one aspect of social order has been addressed. An equally important aspect of order is informal rule following, which is even more difficult to measure and compare. Thus the dearth of empirical comparative studies of social order.

Nevertheless, there are few people who would disagree that Japan has a high level of social order, especially when compared to a country such as the United States (see Rohlen [1989] and Hechter and Kanazawa [1993] for a good overall discussion of this point). Whether too much order is as undesirable as too little order is a question we will consider throughout this book. In general, most people would agree that order is desirable. It would be difficult to imagine living in a society where people do not follow basic rules of conduct. Whether the issue is laws or merely behavioral norms, interaction with others would be very difficult without such order. However, behavioral conformity, when pushed too far, becomes oppressive.

Thus, as mentioned above, social order is a two-edged sword. Although most people would agree that low crime rates are a highly valued social characteristic, it is less clear that normative behavior is equally valued. Most people prefer to live in a society where they know what is appropriate social behavior (though one might also prefer the freedom to not comply). Anyone who has traveled to another country where the norms and mores are different knows how stressful it can be to not know how to act in a given situation. People also appreciate it when others act as they expect them to act. Most people prefer to live in a society where things are predictable: The newspaper will be delivered on time each morning, the train will arrive on time, our coworkers will do their jobs responsibly, and so on. Perhaps in an ideal world, everyone *else* would conform to social norms. Of course, that is not how social order works. The same constraints placed on others that ensure behavioral conformity are also placed on each person. Thus, whereas living in a society with low social order can be frustrating and stressful, living in a society that has mechanisms of control that do not permit deviation from the norms can be equally stressful. Therefore, although social order is generally positive, the issue is complex. There is always a price to be paid for increasing the degree of order in a society.

There are a variety of theoretical approaches possible for understanding social order. The majority of past studies on Asia in general, and Japan specifically, were conducted by anthropologists (see, for example, Benedict [1946]; Smith [1985]; Ben-Ari, Moeran, and Valentine [1990]; Hendry [1993]). Most of these studies are excellent in their own right, but in terms of understanding order, they are of limited use. Social characteristics are often described as either cultural or normative manifestations rather than continuously created and maintained patterns of interaction. Thus, cultural characteristics such as Japan's Confucian past, or normative characteristics such as "group-oriented," "dependent," and "hardworking" are often invoked as explanations of order. These explanations may be technically correct, but they are incomplete as explanations.

Cultural explanations suffer from two shortcomings. First, they do not tend to be sufficient. There are other societies with Confucian origins that differ significantly from Japan. Confucian teachings, which emphasize political stability and respect for the established rulers, did not prevent a Communist revolution in China. More important, it is often forgotten that much of Japan's history is one of regional conflict and peasant uprisings. It is unclear why Confucianism, or any other cultural characteristic, promotes order better now than in the past. This does not mean that religious and cultural values are unimportant, but it suggests that they are not sufficient explanations.

The other limitation of cultural explanations is that they are not specific. Although there is such a thing as "cultural lags," where cultural characteristics continue to exert an influence on modern societies without any supportive social structure, it is more common for cultural characteristics to be maintained through continuing patterns of social interaction (Murakami and Rohlen [1992]; Mouer and Sugimoto [1986]; Harris [1980]; Nakane [1970]). Thus, the degree to which Confucianism promotes order in Japan is likely related to the continued teachings of Confucian principles in schools and through other mediums (such as children's stories and so on). If this is the case, then a more direct explanation of how order is promoted in modern Japan would be through educational materials. There is no reason to invoke the broad and nonspecific term "culture" or even "religion."

Normative explanations also are of limited use, although like cultural explanations, they might be technically correct. Normative explanations tend to overlap with cultural explanations, explaining social order in terms of shared morals and values, and strong group solidarity (see, for example, Gordon [1985]; Maraini [1975]; Doi [1973]; or more generally

Parsons [1937]). The main difference is that normative explanations focus on the internalization of social norms and values through the socialization process. The main problem, as with cultural explanations, is that they do not provide sufficient or precise explanations. Normative expla-' nations are also sometimes tautological. Of course, order exists in Japan because the Japanese people behave normatively. That is, after all, how one measures order. It is akin to claiming the crime rate in Japan is low because people have been socialized to be law abiding. How does one know they are socialized to be law abiding? Because most Japanese do not break the law. Normative explanations also suffer in that they cannot account for variations in social order from one society to another, nor can they account for situational variations in an individual's behavior (Kanazawa [1997]). If behavior is based primarily on internalized norms and values, it should be consistent across a variety of social settings. Yet it is well known that people's behavior is greatly affected by the social context. (See Mouer and Sugimoto [1986] for an excellent critique of these theoretical perspectives.)

A more satisfying explanation assumes that order is continually created and maintained through very specific social processes. An excellent paper that proposed just such an orientation to explain social order in Japan was Thomas Rohlen's "Order in Japanese Society: Attachment, Authority, and Routine" (1989). It was followed by a more formal model proposed first by Hechter, Friedman, and Kanazawa (1992), then by Hechter and Kanazawa (1993), and finally by Kanazawa (1997) that they called the solidaristic theory of social order. This perspective focuses on the interaction of individuals in small groups and proposes that order is an unintentional by-product of this type of interaction. Its orientation is social psychological in nature and focuses on group monitoring and sanctioning. Simply put, each social group (e.g., family, work group, club, and so on) carefully controls the behavior of its members. The purpose is to maintain control over the members' behavior and achieve group goals, but the unintentional consequence is order for the entire society. Although this perspective, too, has some limitations, it proposes a very specific and compelling explanation of social order, and the concept of group monitoring and sanctioning is one important aspect of what we call informal social control. We will now turn to that subject.

Informal Social Control

We use the term social control to refer to whatever methods are used to maintain social order. In the field of criminology, an important distinction is between informal and formal methods of social control (Stark [1998]; Shoham and Hoffmann [1991]). Informal social control has a wide variety of components that run from basic socialization at home and in school to peer pressure and informal group monitoring and sanctioning. The focus is on ways that normative (socially approved) behavior is taught and reinforced in a variety of typical social settings. Formal social control, on the other hand, refers specifically to the criminal justice system, and a society's more formal ways of enforcing social norms that are seen as important enough to have been codified into laws. Although we will discuss formal social control in some detail in Chapter 6, the focus of this book is on informal methods of social control.

We focus on informal social control because it is primarily through this method that social order is produced and maintained in Japan. It is also in this area that Japanese and American societies differ the most. That is not to imply that informal social control does not exist or is not effective in the United States. Despite a very high crime rate, the overwhelming percentage of people follow both the explicit and implicit rules of society. They do so because of informal social control. That is, people have been socialized to follow society's rules, and they interact in social situations where behavioral conformity is rewarded. However, few countries use informal social control methods more effectively than Japan, and throughout this book we will focus on how and why this is the case.

Informal social control involves all of the informal, and sometimes unintentional, ways in which normative behavior is taught and maintained. Normative behavior is typically taught through traditional social institutions such as the family and the education system (Turnbull [1983]; Elkin and Handel [1978]; Abell and Gecas [1997]) and peer influences (McCandless [1969]; Mussen, Conger, and Kagan [1974]), and involves both operant conditioning (i.e., learning through rewards and punishments) and the imitating of others. Normative behavior is typically *maintained* through group monitoring processes (Willer and Anderson [1981]). This can also involve operant conditioning and imitative behavior, but the emphasis is on how closely and effectively the group can observe and sanction (punish) inappropriate behavior (Hechter [1987]).

Informal social control is a very effective way of promoting order in any society, because through the socialization process, social norms and mores are internalized. People obey the rules not because they are forced to, but because they want to. They have accepted many of society's values as their own. Further, through informal group monitoring, inappropriate behavior is quickly detected and punished. When these groups are important social groups (such as a work or social group), individuals tend to comply with group norms since noncompliance might jeopardize their standing in the group. (There are times when group norms and social norms are in conflict, but this is a topic we will discuss later.) Even in a country such as the United States, where individual behavior is fairly heterogeneous, the overwhelming percentage of people follow social norms.

Of course, informal social control is not always effective. There is always variation in the socialization process as well as variation in the ability of groups to monitor and sanction inappropriate behavior. In general, the closer the group, the more effective it is both in instilling group values and in controlling the behavior of its members. That is, when people spend a great deal of time together and group membership is highly valued, behavioral conformity is more easily produced and maintained. We will explore in future chapters how Japan has produced a social structure that does just that.

Finally, we note that although the focus of this book is somewhat different than other books on Japanese society in that it focuses on social psychological principles of small group dynamics, it shares much in common with classic studies of Japanese society. For example, one of the earliest discussions of Japanese society was provided by Ruth Benedict in her classic book *The Chrysanthemum and the Sword* (1946). In it, she characterizes Japan as a "shame culture," while the United States is an example of a "guilt culture." This characterization attracted a fair amount of criticism since the terms appear to be value-laden and somewhat simplistic. However, this early observation is very much consistent with the theoretical model presented in this paper. Benedict's main contention is that behavior in Japan is governed by a fear of being embarrassed or disgraced; that is, a fear that one's behavior might reflect poorly on themselves or on their group. People in the United States, on the other hand, rely more heavily on teaching universal principles (values and norms), and therefore, individual conscience is the main guide for behavior. Thus, when Japanese people behave inappropriately, they feel shame, whereas Americans are more likely to feel guilt. This concept has been controversial since it was first written, with many Westerners using it to brand Japanese as having "situational morality." In fairness to Benedict, she did not appear to attach any values to these terms, and a variety of Japan scholars have defended her characterization (Reischauer [1978]; Lebra [1976]; Tasker [1989]; Taylor [1983]). Reischauer succinctly characterizes this cross-national difference in behavioral restrictions by stating that "To the Westerner the Japanese may seem weak or even lacking in principles; to the Japanese the Westerner may seem harsh and self-righteous in his judgments and lacking in human feelings" (1978, 141).

The language of social anthropology and social psychology differ, but Benedict's main proposition can be restated (we believe a bit more precisely) in terms of small-group interactions. In Japan, behavior is regulated primarily by group monitoring and sanctioning. Given the ubiquitous nature of social groups in Japan and the relative lack of alternative venues of behavioral expression, behavioral conformity is less a product of individual decisions than it is a product of the social structure. This concept will be developed in greater detail in the following chapter. What this book adds to Benedict's original premise is not only a discussion of the specific mechanism that produces behavioral conformity, but also a discussion of the greater social consequences that flow from this type of group dynamics.

The Organization of the Book

This book is divided into four parts. The first part introduces the theoretical orientation used to understand how social order is produced and maintained. As mentioned above, the focus will be social psychological in nature, exploring those characteristics of small-group interactions that successfully promote conforming behavior and discourage nonconforming behavior. We will propose that small-group interaction patterns that emerge within institutions are ultimately responsible, albeit unintentionally, for high social order. That is, as these groups pursue their own goals, they control their members' behavior to the extent that high order at the societal level naturally emerges.

The second part presents concrete examples of how this all occurs. The focus is on how small groups are formed within basic social institutions, and how these institutions encourage certain patterns of interaction within the groups that make it relatively easy for the group to control the behavior of its members. The specific institutions we will discuss are education, work, the family, and the criminal justice system.

The above perspective claims that social order is not intentionally produced in Japan, but naturally arises as an unintended consequence of behavioral conformity at the small-group level. However, high social order is not the only unintended consequence of this form of social structure. The third part discusses other unintended consequences that the Japanese social structure and the nature of social interactions produce. These consequences tend to not only be unintentional, but in many regards, counterintuitive. For example, we will propose that because of the closed nature of small groups and their intense forms of social interaction, Japanese tend to be less trusting of others than are people in many other countries, particularly Americans. This, in turn, has serious political and economic repercussions. We will also claim that the same social structural conditions strongly influence the way religious organizations have developed in Japan, and explain why the Japanese religious landscape is so different from that of the West.

Finally, in our concluding section, Part Four, we speculate on how and why Japanese society, and in particular social institutions, developed the way they did. In this regard, we attempt to answer two questions: how institutions in general emerge, and why Japanese institutions seem to differ in several key characteristics from similar institutions in other countries. As with our theory of social order, we attempt to show that institutions can emerge spontaneously through individual cooperative behavior. We then suggest that Japanese institutions differ from institutions in other countries because of a combination of adaptive processes and historical events.

2

The Solidaristic Theory
of Social Order

Why do some societies have higher levels of order than others?

The problem of order is one of the most fundamental questions in the social sciences, and there has been a renewed interest in the study of social order. Many thoughtful exegeses on the topic (Binmore [1994, 1998]; Elster [1989]; Hampton [1986]; Wrong [1994]), however, fail to offer explanations of social order in the form of empirically testable theory. Moreover, social scientists who do offer empirically testable theories (Ellickson [1991]; Kollock [1993a, 1993b, 1994]; Macy [1989, 1990, 1991a, 1991b]; Orbell and Dawes [1991, 1993]; Ostrom [1990]; Ostrom, Walker, and Gardner [1992]) only purport to explain cooperation in dyads and small groups, not order at the societal level.

In this chapter, we present a theory of social order based on the earlier work of Michael Hechter and his associates (Chai and Hechter [1998]; Hechter [1987, 1989, 1993]; Hechter, Friedman, and Kanazawa [1992]; Hechter and Kanazawa [1993]; Kanazawa [1997]; Kanazawa and Friedman [1999]). To our knowledge, it is the only deductive theory that explains the empirical variations in the levels of social order in large and complex national societies with multiple groups with conflicting and competing goals (which encompass all nation states today, including Japan). Throughout this book, we will use this solidaristic theory of social order to explain how Japanese social groups unintentionally produce a high level of social order in their attempts to increase their own group solidarity. From the perspective of this theory, social order at the societal level is an unintended by-product of the groups' attempts to control their members' behavior in order to achieve their idiosyncratic goals, and of the resultant conformity of members to group norms. We will therefore first present the key elements of this theory in this chapter before we go on in subsequent chapters to demonstrate how the theory explains how Japanese social groups function.

How Social Order Emerges as
an Unintended Consequence of Group Solidarity

We define *social order* as the extent to which individuals comply with important norms of society. (Important norms are those that the state attempts to enforce.) Social order is therefore a societal (macro) level phenomenon, a characteristic of a society, not of individuals or groups within a society. However, mechanisms operative at lower levels of aggregation can generate and then maintain social order. In a sense, the state can delegate the task of generating and maintaining social order to its constituent groups (Hechter, Friedman, and Kanazawa [1992]; Posner [1996]).

The state itself can produce global order if it can monitor the behavior of every single individual at all times in order to induce compliance to norms. Within any large and complex society, however, monitoring and sanctioning all citizens effectively becomes increasingly difficult, and citizens will not necessarily comply with norms voluntarily in the absence of social control. That means that smaller groups in society, such as families, schools, and work organizations, must bear the responsibility of monitoring and sanctioning their respective members in order to induce group members' compliance to norms.

When social control at the group (meso) level is efficient, the result at the societal (macro) level is essentially the same as though the society acted as a single group. If groups are effective as agents of social control and their respective members have higher probability of compliance to group norms as a result, then the society as a whole will consist of individuals who have a higher probability of compliance, *regardless of the actual contents of the norms with which they are complying*. Their higher probabilities of compliance are not owing to their membership in the society, but to their membership in the groups, which function as the actual agents of social control.

We define *group solidarity* as the extent to which a group achieves its goals (Kanazawa [1997, 85, def. 2]). The more successful a group is in achieving its goals, the higher its solidarity. A group's norms are designed to induce members to behave in ways that increase its solidarity; whatever the group's goals are, its norms dictate that members contribute toward the attainment of its goals. Thus, the more compliant members are to group norms, the higher the group solidarity. It follows from this logic that macrolevel social order is a function of mesolevel group solidarities. Ceteris paribus, social order is higher in societies where groups have higher levels of solidarity than in societies where the average level of group solidarity is lower, because more individuals are in compliance with group norms when the average level of solidarity in society is higher.

Not all groups are the same, however. The goals that groups pursue, and thus the type of behavior that compliant individuals exhibit, vary widely. Some groups are *productive* with respect to social order while others are similarly *counterproductive* (Kanazawa [1997]). Productive groups require their members to behave in ways that do not violate the important norms of society, whereas counterproductive groups demand that their members comply with group norms that violate the important norms. Productive, in this sense, means that the group increases social order; counterproductive similarly means that the group decreases social order. The Young Republicans, the Boy Scouts, and the Episcopalians are examples of productive groups. Street gangs, separatist militias, and extreme religious cults are examples of counterproductive groups.

Since social order is the extent to which individuals comply with important norms of society, higher solidarities among counterproductive groups produce individual behavior that threatens social order, and thus reduce rather than enhance order. (Imagine what would happen to social order if street gangs become more successful.) Only higher solidarities among productive groups promote social order. Social order must then also be a function of group productiveness. Therefore, (holding constant the average level of group solidarity in society), social order is higher in societies with more productive and fewer counterproductive groups.

It therefore follows that social order is a multiplicative function of two mesolovel properties of the group: solidarity and productiveness. Figure 2.1 presents the entire theory. Although social order in the solidaristic theory is a joint function of group solidarity and productiveness, in this book we will deal only with how the production of group solidarity, groups' attempts to control the behavior of their members, produce social order as an unintended consequence. We will not explain social order as a function of group productiveness in this book (except to note that some productive groups have both productive and counterproductive norms; see our discussion of how Japanese corporations foster white-collar crime in Chapters 7 and 8). Therefore, we will concentrate only on the group solidarity submodel in the remainder of this chapter and in the book. For our present purposes, it will be sufficient to point out that group productiveness is the extent to which the group's goals are conducive to the production of social order. We will refer readers interested in group productiveness to Hechter, Friedman, and Kanazawa (1992), Kanazawa (1997), and Kanazawa and Friedman (1999).

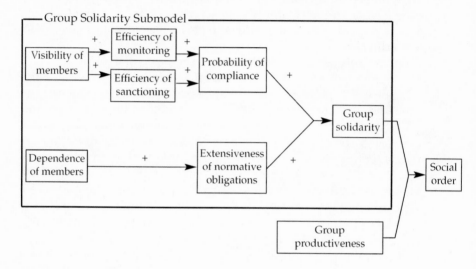

FIGURE 2.1   Solidaristic Theory of Social Order

If social order is a partial function of the solidarity of constituent groups, as Figure 2.1 demonstrates, then the next question is: What determines group solidarity?

How Groups Produce Solidarity

In his classic book, Olson (1965) points out that individuals are rational and self-interested. They will therefore not *voluntarily* sacrifice themselves and work for the good of the group, that is, toward the production of collective goods (goods that benefit all members of the group). Olson argues that if a group is to produce collective goods, its individual members must somehow be induced to contribute toward them. Olson's solution to this problem (known as the collective action problem) is to offer individual members selective incentives, rewards only for those who contribute toward the group's goals. He argues that even rational, self-interested individuals will be motivated to contribute to the group if they value the selective incentives. However, this solution has been shown to be logically flawed. Selective incentives to encourage contribution toward the group are themselves collective goods that must be produced or paid for (Frohlich and Oppenheimer [1970, 120]). Thus the Olsonian solution of the collective action problem through the use of selective incentives assumes a *prior* solution, and merely regresses the theoretical problem.

In order to induce rational, self-interested individuals to comply with group norms and increase solidarity, there must be effective social control mechanisms that monitor individual behavior in order to detect and punish noncompliance as well as reward compliance. Hechter (1987) argues that one mechanism that simultaneously increases both the efficiency of monitoring and the efficiency of sanctioning is visibility. The more visible individual behavior is within the group, the easier it is to detect noncompliance. At the same time, higher visibility also increases the efficiency of sanctioning because sanctioning one individual has a ripple effect on other members when the sanctioning is easily visible to others. Thus higher visibility obviates duplication of sanctioning, and the group can economize on the sanctioning costs.

Consider the typical work environments of white-collar workers in the United States and Japan. In the United States, many white-collar workers have their own offices, with four walls and a door. These workers have complete privacy in their offices when they close their doors. Workers without offices often have cubicles that afford some measure of privacy. Behavior in offices and cubicles is largely undetectable and therefore unaccountable. Workers may not always be in compliance with the company rules (as attested by the number of people who play Solitaire and other computer games on company time).

In contrast, white-collar workers in Japan do not have their own offices. They usually have desks next to each other in a large room. Their supervisors' desks are only a few feet away. The cover photo for this book depicts a typical working environment. Workers are in full view of their colleagues during the entire workday. Colleagues can watch their every move; workers have absolutely no privacy or opportunity to misbehave. If a worker wants to play Solitaire on company time, he must do so in front of all of his colleagues *and bosses*.

Further, if the supervisor were to call one of the workers to reprimand him (possibly for playing Solitaire on company time), the supervisor must do so in front of all of the other workers. Everyone in the large room witnesses the supervisor reprimanding the subordinate. Not only does this negative sanction in public view multiply the humiliation for the subordinate, it more than likely deters other workers from making the same mistake. The same outcome would not happen in the United States, where supervisors are more likely to call delinquent employees into their own office to reprimand them. Other workers usually do not witness a coworker's punishment and therefore miss the opportunity to learn the potential consequences of noncompliance.

Since monitoring and sanctioning are the two pillars of social control, and since effective social control mechanisms induce compliance to norms, the greater efficiency of monitoring and sanctioning, the higher the probability that individuals will comply with the group norms. And since visibility of group members simultaneously increases the efficiency of both monitoring and sanctioning, it follows that visibility increases group solidarity by increasing the probability of compliance (as Figure 2.1 shows).

Another way to increase group solidarity is to increase the extensiveness of normative obligations: the proportion of individual behavior that group norms attempt to regulate. For any given level of compliance, the higher the extensiveness of normative obligations, the more individuals are doing to promote the group goals. A group can thus increase its solidarity by requiring its members to do more toward its goals. How might a group do this?

Hechter (1987) argues that the dependence of members on their group increases the extensiveness of normative obligations. The more dependent the individuals are on their group for the collective goods it provides, the more obligations it can safely impose on them without risking the members leaving the group. The dependence of members set the upper limit to the extensiveness of normative obligations because, if the latter exceeds the former, individuals will simply leave the group and join similar groups in the environment.

Once again, compare the typical white-collar workers in the United States and Japan. American firms cannot make extraordinary demands on their workers, especially off the company clock, because if they did, the workers would simply quit the firm and work for another firm that would make fewer demands on them. The free labor market allows workers to switch jobs and simultaneously prevents firms from increasing the extensiveness of normative obligations on the part of workers beyond a certain point. Workers are not very heavily dependent on any given firm. This is especially true of highly valued employees since they tend to be the most marketable and can easily change jobs. Thus, if an American firm demands too much from its workers, it tends to drive away the best employees and retain the worst.

In contrast, many white-collar workers in Japan have lifetime employment. Although this system provides unparalleled job security, it simultaneously means that workers cannot switch jobs easily once their career begins at one firm. Because most major companies have the lifetime employment system in place, few would hire those in midcareer. That means that Japanese white-collar workers simply cannot quit their job, no matter how much they hate it, because they would not be able to find another job if they did. This total dependence of Japanese white-collar workers on their jobs allows the companies to place extensive normative obligations on their workers, often beyond their normal working hours. And, in sharp contrast to the United States, highly-valued workers in Japan are *more* dependent on their company, rather than less, because they have achieved their higher status within their firm and would forfeit that status by quitting (since starting a new job, if at all possible, usually means starting over within the corporate hierarchy).

Although both the probability of compliance and the extensiveness of normative obligations are important determinants of group solidarity, either one alone is insufficient. If the former is high and the latter is low, individuals will be complying with the very few obligations that the group imposes on them. If the former is low and the latter is high, then the group imposes many normative obligations on its members, but they need not comply with them. Under either scenario, the group is not likely to achieve many of its goals, and solidarity remains low. The production of group solidarity requires that both the probability of compliance and the extensiveness of normative obligations be high.

The group solidarity submodel of the solidaristic theory of social order therefore explains group solidarity as a multiplicative (joint) function of visibility and dependence of group members. The more visible group members are within the group, and the more dependent they are on the group for the collective benefits it provides for the members, the higher the solidarity of the group. Then, *as long as the groups are productive* (i.e., conventional in their goals), their higher solidarities have the unintended consequence of increasing the overall level of social order. The group attempts to control the behavior of its members, not to increase the level of social order, but to increase its solidarity, so that the group can induce more of its members to comply with group norms more of the time, and hence achieve more of its goals. But social order at the macro level nonetheless emerges from this process of group conformity.

Conclusion

The solidaristic theory explains social order at the macro (societal) level as a partial function of group solidarities at the meso level. The higher the levels of group solidarity in society, the higher the level of social order. Thus groups unintentionally contribute toward the production of social order when they monitor and control the behavior of their members to make sure that they comply with group norms. In Part Two, we will explore how the higher visibility of the Japanese within their groups and their greater dependence on their groups produce higher levels of solidarity for their groups, and hence the higher level of social order. Then, in Part Three, we will argue that the same institutions of higher visibility and dependence also produce other unintended consequences quite unrelated (or even contrary) to social order.

PART TWO

Social Institutions

3

The Education System: Social Initiation

Much has been written, both positive and negative, about the Japanese education system. Ironically, much praise of the education system comes from abroad, whereas the Japanese themselves have been very self-critical. We will not review the pluses and minuses of the education system, as they are well known (see, for example, Rohlen [1983] for the best overall discussion of the topic). Suffice it to say that the Japanese education system differs in many regards from the American education system, and the differences cannot be easily described as better or worse. At the kindergarten and elementary school level, Japanese schools emphasize overall socialization more than their American counterparts, and at the middle school and high school level the Japanese emphasize more rote memorization and acquiring test-taking skills than their American counterparts. Nevertheless, the purpose of this chapter is not to give a complete description of the Japanese education system, nor is it to assess the system in terms of its accomplishments or failings. We are primarily concerned with how the education system contributes to social order. Therefore, we focus exclusively on the characteristics related to the model presented in the previous chapter; that is, we will discuss issues of dependence and visibility, and how they lead to normative obligations and an effective monitoring and sanctioning system.

Before turning to this discussion, though, we should note that juvenile delinquency, particularly juvenile criminal behavior, has recently been on the rise in Japan and has generated a great deal of attention in the popular press. However, compared to other countries, juvenile crime and delinquency is still quite low. Table 3.1 displays recent statistics provided by the United Nations on the number of juveniles arrested on suspicion of committing a crime. It is difficult to compare any type of crime statistics cross-nationally because of differences in definitions, enforcement

TABLE 3.1   Juvenile Suspects per 100,000 Population

Country	Juvenile Suspects
United States	848
Canada	435
Austria	311
Sweden	247
Republic of Korea	244
France	189
Denmark	150
Russian Federation	136
Japan	105

SOURCE: Fifth United Nations Survey of Crime Trends and Operations of Criminal Justice Systems (1995).

patterns, and record keeping. However, assuming that these figures provide a rough estimate of juvenile problems in each country, it is clear that Japan enjoys a relatively low number of juvenile offenders per capita.

We will now turn to a discussion of why so many young people in Japan conform to social norms and behavioral expectations, and how the school system contributes to this conformity.

Dependence and Normative Obligations

We can conceive of dependence as arising from two very different sources. First, dependence can be taught and fostered through socialization practices that encourage and reward dependent behavior. Second, dependence can be the natural outcome of a system that provides no alternative means of achieving a desired goal. Both are applicable to Japan, and we will discuss each separately.

Socialization

Psychologists and social scientists have observed that the goal of early childhood socialization differs in Japan and the United States. Americans tend to view children as born totally dependent and the socialization process is aimed at promoting independence. Japanese, however, view children as born independent, and the socialization process is aimed at gradually drawing the child into the social group (Doi [1973]; Lebra [1976]). Thus, it is noted by these scholars, a central part of the socialization process in Japan is to foster a sense of group dependence. This certainly appears to be true, even if most researchers misunderstand its cause. There is a general sense, largely based on the work of Doi, that this desire to foster a sense of dependence is somehow deeply rooted in the psychological makeup of the Japanese. However, socialization of children in any society is done with the explicit purpose of preparing children for entry into society. The fact that Japanese socialization fosters dependence while American socialization fosters independence is because these characteristics will ultimately aid them in their respective societies. In other words, it is a bit misleading to state that Japanese adults are dependent on social groups because they were socialized to be that way. It is more accurate to state that children are socialized to be dependent on social groups because the Japanese social structure is designed to reward that behavior in adults.

Nevertheless, it is true that dependence is fostered from a very early time in the socialization process. Furthermore, this emphasis is not only seen in parenting strategies (e.g., putting a child in a crib or separate room as opposed to sleeping in the same bed with a child), but can also be seen in early schooling practices (Lewis [1988]; Hendry [1986]; Peak [1987]). Peak (1989, 1987) reports that preschool teachers consistently consider nonparticipation in group activities the most serious behavioral problem a preschooler can have. Indeed, preschool and kindergarten teachers see their primary task as socializing children into group activities. A survey of kindergarten teachers in the United States and Japan illustrates this goal, as well as points to an important difference in early socialization practices in the two countries. U.S. teachers consistently list as their primary objective increasing a child's self-esteem and self-reliance. Japanese teachers, on the other hand, consistently list concern for others and enjoying activities with friends as the primary lesson they want their children to learn. Catherine Lewis (1988), in her excellent study of Japanese elementary schools, notes similar findings. When asked what the most important lesson is for first graders to learn, the great majority of Japanese teachers answered group relationships (i.e., making friends, getting along well with others, and so on).

Because of the importance placed on learning social skills, a wide range of activities and behaviors are permitted to the extent that they promote social learning. Thus, kindergarten and elementary school classes are often characterized by a great deal of noise and commotion (at least when compared with classes in the United States) (Peak [1989]). This is permitted because it is believed that children, if given the freedom, will naturally form friendships and develop social relations. It is important to remember that from a Japanese teacher's point of view, running about and playing with the other children does not take time away from the lesson plan; playing *is* the lesson plan. Japanese teachers firmly believe that the key to future success hinges on the child learning to enjoy school and especially social relations with the other students. Social relations are the foundation on which everything else is built. The student who enjoys school and is a good group member will eventually do well in academics, and more generally, in society. Along these lines, Rohlen notes, "At the beginning of each stage of schooling a great deal is made of the closeness, friendships, and happy togetherness . . . that children will experience. Much effort and ingenuity goes into establishing a strong identity between the child, the class as a whole, and the small group to which the child belongs" (1989, 25–26). Furthermore, strong group identification will result in more effective use of peer pressure to maintain behavioral conformity throughout the student's school life.

Even fighting, a behavior that might be thought of as the antithesis of developing good social relations, is seen as an important aspect of socializing children into the group. Peak (1989) quotes the following passage from a 1982 booklet presented to schools by the Tokyo Board of Education:

> Fights between children are an important experience in acquiring proper social attitudes and behavior. Through fights, children communicate their own needs and desires to others, come to accept others' needs and desires, and learn the rules of child society.
>
> If from the time that children are small, parents involve themselves too much saying "don't fight," "play together nicely," and "take turns," children are deprived of natural opportunities to bump up against each other. In that case, children come running to tattle "so and so is teasing me." Doesn't it too often happen that the parent then takes the child under their wing and solves the dispute?
>
> When children fight, watch the fight and allow it to happen. Through fighting, children come to understand others' viewpoints, learn tolerance and self-restraint and self-assertiveness. It is important to raise your child so that he has plenty of experience in the normal fights that occur in everyday life. (107–108)

Attempts at socializing children into the group are neither confined to preschool nor are they merely an implicit educational goal. Socializaton is an *explicit* part of the school curriculum. Although most Western school curricula emphasize academic subjects, the Japanese Ministry of Education mandates that all school curricula contain three categories: academic subjects, moral education, and special group-centered activities (Kida [1986]; Okihara [1986]). Moral education seeks to teach respect for one's family, school, and community, and the group-centered activities seek to promote a sense of belonging and commitment to the group. Thus, fostering a group identity, and by extension a sense of psychological group dependence, is an explicit part of the national school curriculum.

An excellent example of an early schooling experience that draws students into the group, thereby fostering a sense of dependence, is the way in which first graders are treated on the first day of elementary school. In the United States there is no special ceremony; the students merely report to their classrooms. However, in Japan it is a special occasion. Preparation begins in the family where the child is bought special clothes to begin school (either in the form of a uniform if the school requires one, or merely dress clothes if there is no uniform). The child is also given a special day pack that all students use to carry their schoolwork back and forth to school. It is common for relatives to send money and telegrams congratulating the child. On the first day of school, the parents accompany the child to the school, where the child is greeted by school officials and other employees who bow deeply and offer their own congratulations. At the school entrance the children's names are listed on the walls so they can see which class they are in and who their classmates will be (many of whom they attended kindergarten with).

All of the students in the school congregate in the school auditorium, but the first graders occupy the place of honor, sitting apart from everyone in the very front. An elaborate ceremony then takes place with teachers and officials making speeches to welcome the new students. This welcome also includes music, songs, and picture taking. Then, one by one, representatives from each of the other grades stand and welcome the first graders, inviting them to join the older children in play or ask questions of them if they have any problems. Finally, the ceremony ends and students are escorted to their new classroom by the older students and are assigned desks and seats.

It is interesting to note that, by comparison, graduation ceremonies are very quiet and subdued. Unlike the United States, which tends to celebrate "completion," Japanese celebrate "beginnings." For many, graduation is seen as a sad time because it marks the end of many friendships (Rohlen [1983]). It is telling that at nearly all graduations throughout Japan it is traditional to sing "Auld Lang Syne," a nostalgic song about days gone by, rather than talk about the future. This is, of course, consistent with the importance placed on group identity above and beyond individual achievement.

The point is that through a variety of activities and pedagogical tools, children are socialized into a group setting where they develop a strong sense of identity and belonging. The list of activities that serve to reinforce this is impressive. Not only do students wear matching clothes and work, eat, and play together in the same classroom throughout the year, but they even perform the majority of janitorial work, cleaning the rooms and hallways, washing walls, and picking up trash (Nishio [1985]; Okihara [1986]). Thus the students develop a sense of ownership: they are not just attending a school, but rather, this is *their* school. Of course many schools also require students to wear uniforms, which further promotes a strong sense of school identity.

Thus, at a relatively early age, Japanese schoolchildren come to view themselves as members of a group. The actual number and size of the groups one feels dependent on tends to grow over time into a series of expanding concentric circles. Students first learn to form friendships with several classmates, and perform a variety of classroom functions as small groups. They later come to see themselves as members of the class, then the school, and eventually the community and society. As Rohlen (1983) writes:

> The foundation of the American notion of maturation lies in its focus on ex-
> perience, choice and judgment. We make our own destinies and are respon-
> sible for our own choices, therefore our young need to practice making up
> their own minds. . . . In Japan, maturation centers on the process of integra-
> tion into the larger society. Shifting first from the dependency and intimacy
> of infancy into family group membership and then to generalized social
> roles and group membership in school leads to adulthood, as defined by in-
> tegration into work organizations and parenting roles. (280)

Lack of Alternatives

As stated above, being socialized into a group is only one way in which a person develops a sense of group dependence. One is also dependent on the group to the extent that the group is necessary for success. For exam-ple, if a politician must join a political party in order to be included on a ballot in an upcoming election, then that politician is dependent on the political party, regardless of whether he or she has been socialized to be a good party member. There is no alternative way to achieve the desired goal. Thus, dependence might exist quite apart from any socializing in-fluences, if the social system does not provide alternatives to group membership.

This issue becomes more relevant as the student grows older. From ju-nior high school on, the school curriculum changes, focusing more and more intensely on acquiring academic skills. Of course, this occurs dur-ing early adolescence, a time when greater behavioral problems typi-cally arise. At this point, students begin to enjoy school less. A survey conducted by the Japanese Ministry of Education found that although 91 percent of elementary school students were satisfied with school life, that number declined to 70 percent and then 64 percent for junior and high school students, respectively (Monbusho [1998]). However, at the same time that school becomes less enjoyable, students begin to understand and appreciate the importance of doing well in school. The basic message students learn from junior high school on is that one must work hard and do what one is told, or suffer severe consequences (Rohlen [1992]).

Unlike the United States, where students typically attend neighborhood schools until they reach college age, Japanese students must take high school entrance exams. The exams determine which high schools they will attend, and high schools vary greatly in how well they train their students to take the college entrance exam. The best high schools are able to place many of their students in top universities, and private companies as well as civil service agencies hire new workers based almost exclusively on the quality of university attended. It is very difficult for a person not attending a good university to obtain a good job. (See the extensive literature on educational tracking in Japan, e.g., Ojima and Miller [1992]; Tsukahara et al. [1990]; Fujita [1985]; Imada and Hara [1979].) Thus, at a fairly young age, Japanese adolescents are made aware of the consequences of not performing well in school. In essence, school work will determine Japanese students' entire future. In other words, there are no alternatives to success other than through good academic performance. Thus, behavioral conformity can still be expected based on dependence, but the dependence is no longer purely psychological, a function of socialization; it is now enforced by pragmatism. There is no other route to success other than by following school rules and doing what one is told.

It is important here to note that decisions concerning entry into elite high schools (and therefore into elite colleges) are not based entirely on academic achievements. One cannot be a "troublemaker" and still be admitted into a top high school based on high test scores alone. One must also win the favor of one's teachers. Mouer and Sugimoto (1986) write:

> One practice which is fairly standard in both private and public schools is the keeping of *naishinsho* (confidential appraisals of the students). In addition to performance in the entrance examination, high schools also consult the *naishinsho* from an applicant's middle school. Teachers are free to write their own feelings about a student. Inquisitive students in good standing with a teacher may receive some comment like "healthy curiosity" or "an exploring mind" whereas those seen as questioning the teacher or disrupting the class will be labeled impertinent. Students are thus in a position of having to calculate what a particular teacher may write on their *naishinsho* before acting. From an early age, attempts are made to remove spontaneity from their behavior. The control mechanism here is not shame, but rather the threat that the door to upward mobility will be closed to them. (258)

Once in high school, the situation becomes somewhat less subjective in that college admittance really is based entirely on test scores. Nevertheless, teachers still remain influential; they are the people training the students to do well on these tests. Certainly it makes good sense to keep relations positive. A teacher who takes a special interest in a student might spend more energy helping that student or recommend additional study materials that will give him or her an advantage over the other students. Thus, high school students must constantly consider the consequences of their behavior and calculate what strategies will best help them perform well on the all-important college entrance exam. Rohlen (1983), therefore, refers to entrance exams as "the dark engine driving high school culture" (317). He further contends that without pressure to perform well on the exams, schools would be far less orderly and students far less conforming.

If college entrance exams are primarily responsible for producing the high social order and conformity exhibited in high schools, what about students who are not college bound? Certainly a great many students display no ability or desire to attend college. It turns out that even for those who do not excel in academics, there is a practical reason to display other socially desirable qualities such as persistence and responsibility. The reason is that high school graduates do not normally go on the job market themselves. Rather, they rely on the school to help place them in their first job. Students who impress their teachers will be nominated for the best jobs. The typical pattern is that a company will notify the school that they are seeking to employ a certain number of high school graduates, and the school then submits a list of the students it recommends (Rohlen [1983]; Rosenbaum and Kariya [1989]). So even students who are not college bound are still very much dependent on their teachers and the school, perhaps even more so than the college-bound students.

It is useful here to note that the above discussion focuses primarily on males in the Japanese education system. This is intentional since in general males are a greater threat to social order in any society (a topic we will take up in detail in later chapters). However, this does not mean females are not dependent on the education system. Owing to structural impediments, far fewer females than males pursue professional careers, but there are still ample reasons to seek success in school. First, although many career paths are blocked, not all are. It is possible for a woman to develop a successful career, even though it is more difficult for her than it is for a man. And for women as well as men, graduating from a top university is a necessity. Also, college is a good place to meet a future spouse, and the better the college, the better job that future spouse is likely to have (Brinton [1993]). Similarly, for women not planning to attend a college, being a good high school student and winning the favor of one's teacher is important since it will lead to a job (albeit a temporary one) in a good company where one can also meet potential spouses. Thus, even though many career paths for females are effectively blocked, getting into a good college or being recommended for a good job by a high school teacher is still a commonly sought goal. This means females are also dependent on the education system.

A Matter of Time

Throughout this discussion, it is possible to lose sight of an even more elementary reason why pressure to perform well in high school curbs delinquent behavior. The students simply do not have time to get into trouble. A recent survey of American high school students found that, on average, they go out with their friends three to four nights a week, and only study four hours a week (National Center for Educational Statistics [1996]), whereas Japanese students rarely socialize in the evenings, and spend, on average, nearly four hours a *day* studying. Moreover, the school year is much longer in Japan than in the United States, and students also attend classes every other Saturday. It is also important to note that more than half of all Japanese students attend after-school clubs and most students also attend after-school *juku* ("cram schools" that help students prepare to take high school and college entrance exams). Tasker (1989) reports that nearly 90 percent of students in the Tokyo area attend a *juku,* and virtually 100 percent of all students admitted to top universities studied at a *juku.*

A recent survey of 2,397 students at thirteen high schools in the Hyogo prefecture (of which Kobe is the best known city) asked students if they participated in any after-school study programs while they were in elementary school or junior high school (Ojima et al. [1998]). The results are presented in Table 3.2. As can be seen, even in elementary school, the majority of people attended a study *juku.* By the third year of middle school, almost 70 percent were attending a *juku,* and about 84 percent were participating in some type of high school preparatory activity.

As can be seen, Japanese students, from a very early age, have very little free time. It is also worth noting that, unlike their American counterparts, Japanese high school students do not drive cars, since the minimum driving age is eighteen. So with almost no free time, and only public transportation to rely on, the majority of young Japanese people (especially males, who are more likely than females to attend a *juku*) have little opportunity to get into trouble.

So far we have discussed a lack of alternatives only as it relates to occupational success. Good jobs can only be had by students able and willing to endure the many hours required to learn the information contained on

TABLE 3.2   Percent of Students Who Studied in After-School Programs While in
Elementary School and Junior High School

School	Juku	Private Tutor	Home Study Program	None
Elementary School	57.2	7.6	18.2	—
Junior High School				
First Year	59.9	4.7	12.8	28.0
Second Year	63.6	7.6	12.8	23.0
Third Year	68.6	14.7	13.0	16.4

SOURCE: Research on the Change in Career Plans of High School Seniors,
Osaka University of Economics (1997 [see Ojima et al. 1998]).

college entrance exams, or at the very least, have pleased their high
school teachers enough to earn a nomination from them for a decent job.
However, one can conceive of many other examples where the Japanese
social structure exhibits a lack of alternatives. Consider what happens after someone enters a university. Whereas in the United States one can,
with relative ease, transfer to a different university, it is extremely difficult to do so in Japan. Similarly, in the United States one can choose to
leave college and return sometime in the future. This is also difficult to
do in Japan. Japanese students are expected to apply for college at age
eighteen, and attend from age nineteen to twenty-three. One cannot decide to leave college and then return at age twenty-five or older (as is
common in the United States). Indeed, once a major is chosen (typically
in one's sophomore year), it is almost impossible to change. Japanese students learn from a fairly early age that once a decision is made, they will
have to live with it. Changes of heart are rarely tolerated and second
chances are rarely granted.

At a more basic level, the same lack of alternatives exists in one's social
life. People rarely choose their primary groups (at least, not after kindergarten). Once groups are established, whether they are friendship
groups, study groups, or work groups, people are expected to be long-
term, loyal members. There are, of course, natural times to leave a group,
such as when a person moves, or graduates school, or is transferred to a
different job location. But one does not typically leave a group because
one is unhappy in that group or seeks to find a better group. Such behavior is seen as socially inappropriate, and would probably lead to social
isolation since established groups do not often take in members who
have abandoned their previous groups (Rohlen [1992]; Nakane [1970]).
Even something as trivial as joining an after-school sports or hobby club
involves a serious commitment that cannot easily be broken. Once stu-

dents join such a club, they are expected to devote considerable time and energy to the club, and not leave until they graduate from the school.

Normative Obligations

The point of all this is that a lack of alternatives means a greater dependence on the group. And, of course, with dependence comes normative obligations. Because students are so dependent on schools, they have little choice but to follow the rules and conform to normative expectations. And normative expectations cover a wide range of a student's academic and private life. For example, most schools have very rigid dress codes as well as rules concerning acceptable hairstyles and the use of makeup. Rules also extend to out-of-school behavior, specifying the ways students ought to spend their free time, and even how one ought to get to and from school (for example, what types of bicycles and helmets are acceptable). Even after-school clubs have a long list of normative obligations associated with them. Clubs are typically run by the students themselves, but are nevertheless extremely demanding and hierarchical. Each club member must treat the older members with deference and do the least desirable work. For example, a student joining a tennis club might not be able to actually play tennis the first year, but instead merely chase balls for the more senior students and then clean the grounds afterward.

Students endure these obligations because of dependence, dependence that has been taught through socialization and that arises through a lack of behavioral options. Yet it is important to remember that this does not necessarily mean the system is coercive (in the sense that students are forced into an inequitable social arrangement). The system persists largely because the group can offer its members tangible rewards. High school teachers *can* help their students find jobs, and good test scores *will* get a student admitted to a top college. Furthermore, in the case of clubs, junior members will soon become senior members, and will enjoy the benefits of a higher place in the hierarchy. In other words, the Japanese social structure is not based on coercion, per se, but on a type of generalized exchange system where members can expect to eventually receive rewards commensurate with their investment.

Yuki (1998, 1996) refers to this type of exchange, which is common in many areas of Japanese society, as "transrelational reciprocity," while Yamagishi et al. (1998) refer to it as "bounded generalized exchanges." The system does promote reciprocity, but the person from whom one receives a favor is often not the person one granted a favor to, and often one must wait a considerable time before eventually receiving those favors. Kumon (1992) makes a similar point when he refers to Japan as a "network society" where long-term relations characterized by a generalized exchange system work at virtually all levels of society. He writes, "Taken in part, this relationship is asymmetric, if not necessarily hierarchical. But, as a whole, it comprises a multilateral relationship of mutual dependence and caretaking in which one plays the role of a dependent on someone at one time, and the role of a caretaker for someone else at another time" (123). Thus, although it is true that dependence on a group instills the group with power, and that power can be used to enforce strict rules of behavior, dependence can only be maintained as long as the group is able to deliver on its promises of future rewards.

Visibility, Monitoring, and Sanctioning

As the model in Chapter 2 suggests, group dependence and normative obligations only lead to behavioral conformity (and ultimately high social order) if members' behavior is visible to others so that inappropriate behavior can be monitored and sanctioned. That is, it must be possible to catch and punish transgressors. It is in this sense that visibility is so important.

In general, public schools in any country are places of high visibility. However, there are a variety of reasons why visibility (as well as monitoring and sanctioning) are higher in Japan than elsewhere. First, there is no free time for students—no independent study periods, free library time, and so on. All students attend class with their teachers all of the time (Rohlen [1983]). And, with the exception of art, music, and physical education classes, the students remain in the same classrooms all day. This includes lunchtime. Although American students will either pack a lunch and eat out on the school grounds or go to a school cafeteria, Japanese students eat in their classrooms alongside their classmates and teacher. Also, as mentioned earlier, after-school clubs and *juku* are extremely popular, so visibility typically extends into the early evening.

Interestingly, even the teachers are in a high visibility environment. Of course, they are with their students much of the day, but when they are not, all of the teachers share a cramped teachers' room. It is common, as we will discuss in the next chapter, for one's work environment to afford no privacy.

High visibility places individuals in positions where other group members can monitor and sanction (i.e., punish) inappropriate behavior. This monitoring and sanctioning process is well developed throughout Japanese society, including at school. Researchers studying Japanese kindergartens and elementary schools often note the heavy reliance on informal social sanctioning by peers to promote appropriate behavior (Hendry [1986]; Lewis [1984, 1989]). For example, Lewis (1989), in her observations of fifteen first-grade classrooms, notes how each day two children assume the role of classroom monitors and are in charge of bringing the class to order and maintaining discipline. Further, when serious discipline problems erupt, the teacher typically asks the class to discuss the behavior and decide on an appropriate punishment. Hendry (1986), in her study of kindergartens in the Tokyo area, makes similar observations:

> Ultimately more important than threats made by the teacher is the pressure to conform which builds up within the peer group itself. At the beginning of the day, when the teacher plays the piano for the children to sit down, it is the children, not she, who grow impatient with the stragglers. Particularly at break and lunchtime, there is little sympathy for those who keep the whole group waiting. In sorting out quarrels, teachers appeal to other children to decide who should apologise. . . . Again they are learning self-control, this time in the interest of the peer group of which they have become part. . . . In many cases, children in Japan remain with the same peer group throughout the period of compulsory education. If the kindergarten is successful in establishing the importance of the identity of this group, teachers in the later stages should have few discipline problems. (57)

A particularly clear example of informal social sanctioning by peers involves the *hanseikai*. It is common for junior and senior high school classes to set aside about fifteen minutes at the end of each day for a time of "reflection and contrition." During these meetings, the teacher usually sits quietly at the front of the classroom while classmates discuss each other's behavior, sometimes praising socially appropriate behavior, but more commonly chastising inappropriate behavior. In other words, students are expected to monitor one another's behavior throughout the day and report to the class any inappropriate behavior that they observed. The accused then usually stands and apologizes to the class. Obviously, such a daily practice is a direct and powerful way of increasing peer pressure to conform.

Monitoring and sanctioning continues throughout middle school and high school. It is not unusual, for example, for teachers to keep a lookout to be sure students return directly to their homes after school. An even closer eye is kept on female high school students, who might be chastised for something as minor as stopping at a convenience store for a soda on the way home. The fact that a school's authority extends beyond school boundaries is evidenced by the fact that many schools have rules concerning what part-time or summer jobs their students are allowed to take. This exercise of authority beyond the boundaries of the school is seen as appropriate and, for the most part, acceptable to both school administrators and students because of the strong sense of group identity fostered by the Japanese system. Students (and teachers) are not merely attending a school, they are representatives of the school. It is, after all, *their school*. And students are often reminded of this. For example, before vacations school assemblies are held and the students are reminded that they have a social responsibility to the school and that any bad behavior not only reflects poorly on themselves, but also on the school and their fellow classmates (Rohlen [1983]).

Given this relationship, it is not surprising that the cost associated with delinquent behavior can be severe. Several years ago a television news program ran a story about a high school soccer team. The team had just won the national high school championship and was scheduled to represent Japan in the upcoming Asian High School Games to be held in South Korea. Unfortunately for the team, during a celebration party after the championship, many of the team members drank beer (the legal drinking age in Japan is twenty), and the local police were notified. If this had occurred in the United States, every effort would have been made to identify the individuals who drank alcohol and punish them (perhaps by removing them from the team). This was not the course of action chosen by the school authorities in Japan. Rather than punishing the individuals, or even the team, the school was prohibited from participating in any national sports events for two years. This type of story is not exceptional. Similar incidents occur regularly, often in connection with the biannual national high school baseball tournament. If a student from one of the participating high schools gets into trouble (for example, is caught fighting or stealing), the high school is expected to withdraw from the tournament, even if the offending student is not a member of the team.

From an American perspective, this might seem harsh and unfair. From a Japanese perspective, however, an individual's actions are never divorced from his or her social context. People are almost always members of groups, and their behavior is attributed as much to the group as it is the individual. Just as employees represent their companies in all actions, both public and private, students represent their schools. Furthermore, the group is responsible for controlling the behavior of its members. In the example presented above concerning the soccer team, the high school failed to prevent the students from participating in inappropriate behavior. It is only natural, therefore, for the high school to be held responsible.

This type of sanctioning is not only seen as appropriate, it is also, more importantly, extremely effective. Although a person contemplating committing a delinquent act might be willing to run the risk of being personally caught and punished, it is quite another issue to run the risk of having one's friends or family punished. Thus, a strong sense of group identity also increases the effectiveness of this form of monitoring and sanctioning.

Conclusion

It is important not to lose sight of the similarities that exist between Japan and other societies. Dependence, normative obligations, monitoring, and sanctioning exist in all societies, and every society's school system punishes noncompliance. The difference is not so much in the types of social controls that exist in Japan, but rather the degree to which they exist. Unfortunately, by focusing on the degree to which dependence, normative obligations, monitoring, and sanctioning exist, an almost Orwellian picture of the Japanese social structure emerges. But such a caricature is very misleading. The great majority of Japanese do not view this system of social control as overly oppressive and controlling. Although an overwhelming majority of people are unhappy with the college examination process, they are generally happy with the basic group structure of social life, including school life. Whereas it is true that group dependence and normative obligations are high in Japan, the social rewards one can reap are also high. From an American perspective, many of the normative expectations described above seem excessive. However, there is a psychological comfort in knowing exactly how to behave and what behavior is expected. There is an impressive amount of sociological literature, rooted originally in Emile Durkheim's concept of anomie, which details the many behavioral problems that arise when social norms are not clearly defined. Anomie is not a serious problem in Japan.

It is instructive to think of a tight-knit church community as an analogy to group life in Japan. Such a community often operates in a fairly closed social environment, with members encouraged to "fellowship" with other members of the church. The explicit reason is to support and encourage one another to live "a good Christian life." In other words, it is an environment with strong normative obligations and high visibility, where inappropriate behavior is monitored and sanctioned. But, of course, in return the members receive a great many social benefits, and most members believe the benefits outweigh the costs.

Judging the overall merits and demerits of the Japanese educational system is complex and subjective. However, its contribution to social order is less ambiguous. Group identity and dependence are carefully fostered through early socialization practices, and later reinforced by a system that does not afford opportunities to succeed outside of established channels. High visibility then allows group members to monitor one another's behavior and sanction inappropriate behavior. The result is high levels of behavioral conformity and, ultimately, high levels of social order. Whether the school system is equally adept at attaining its academic goals is a topic we will leave to others.

4

Work: A Continuation

Our intention in this chapter is not to assess Japanese work patterns or managerial techniques in terms of economic or quality of life successes or failings. A great many books have been published that attempt to make such assessments. Indeed, a rash of books appear every couple of years on this topic, either critical of Japanese work practices or extolling their virtues, depending on the relative strength of the Japanese economy at the time of writing. Our purpose is rather to explore how the organization of work contributes to overall social order in Japanese society. As in the previous chapter, our discussion will focus on issues of dependence and visibility, and how they lead to normative obligations and an effective monitoring and sanctioning system.

It would not be too much of an exaggeration to claim that Chapter 3 could be inserted here changing only the word "school" to the word "work." In many ways, work life, at least for males, is a direct extension of school life. Or perhaps more accurately, school life is a precursor to work life. By stressing social relations, individual responsibility, group loyalty, and a strong sense of school allegiance, schools are essentially training children to become good workers. Further, the whole examination process, which has been soundly criticized for its emphasis on rote memorization over critical thinking, is geared to determine who will best fit in to the current work structure. Both Fallows (1989) and van Wolferen (1989) make this point cogently:

> Few people in Japan contend that the tests are primarily measures of "ability" or "intelligence." Instead, the tests are straightforward measures of memorized information. No one seems interested in discussing whether the knowledge measured on the tests is related to skills that will later prove valuable on the job. That's not what the tests are about: they are measures of determination and effort, pure and simple, so the pointlessness of their content actually enhances their value as tests of will. (Fallows [1989, 45])

That they absorb next to nothing after a couple of hours of cramming is im-
material: they show the world that they are in earnest and have the required
endurance. (van Wolferen [1989, 88])

The point that both authors make is that school and the examination
system encourage students to display their determination, endurance,
and willingness to meet institutional obligations without questioning the
value or meaning of those obligations. In short, people who perform well
on exams will likely be hardworking, conforming, and loyal employees.
The fact that they have not learned any real knowledge that will aid them
in the future is irrelevant. They have displayed the capacity to learn
whatever it is the company teaches them and to faithfully adhere to
whatever policies the company imposes, whether or not the individual
finds those policies rational or meaningful.

Once a person is hired by a company, much of the same characteristics
that led to behavioral conformity at the school, that is, dependence and
visibility, similarly operate at the company level. Murakami and Rohlen
(1992) list a variety of characteristics of large Japanese companies, including the following: lifetime employment; seniority-based wage and promotion; elaborate welfare, bonus, and other benefits; small-group activities; and intensive training and socialization. We will now consider how
these characteristics contribute to social order, and also how smaller companies use similar techniques to create dependence and visibility among
employees.

Dependence and Normative Obligations

Thomas Rohlen (1974) notes that although in the past the main social en-
tity in Japan was the village, now it is the company. Although he wrote
this quite a few years ago, his observation still rings true. A person's social identity and friendship network is largely determined by his or her
place of employment. Company affiliation also has a strong influence on
issues such as marriage, credit, housing, and so on. In that the labor force
is still largely male dominated (especially permanent, career-track positions), this sense of identity and the accompanying dependence is more
true for males than for females. Nevertheless, females also develop a social identity and acquire social status based largely on their husband's occupation, so company dependence extends beyond the individual male
employee to include his family (Brinton [1989]). We might also reiterate
that in terms of social order, males commit the overwhelming percentage
of crimes. Therefore, the degree to which males are restrained by social
control mechanisms is more important to overall social order than the degree to which females are restrained.

In the previous chapter we conceptualized dependence as arising from two different sources: a sense of dependence that is fostered through socialization practices and dependence that is the natural result of a lack of alternatives for success. Although it might seem that socialization influences are confined to early childhood, and therefore less important when looking at work group dependence, this is not the case. Socialization still plays an important role in fostering work group dependence. Therefore, we will begin with a discussion of socialization.

Socialization

First and foremost, we should keep in mind that socialization practices that took place in childhood still have an effect on adult behavior. The intensive training in group behavior and group dynamics influence adult behavior by creating a pattern of social interactions that is hard to break. Also, the internalization of social values that support normative behavior continues to influence behavioral decisions in adulthood. By the time a person enters the workforce, that person has already developed a social self as well as a self-image. Therefore, behavioral patterns tend to be relatively consistent over time.

In addition, companies tend to spend a great deal of time resocializing new employees, reinforcing some social norms, and creating new values and loyalties. As in education, it is instructive to look at how new employees are greeted and inducted into the company. The parallels to the example given in Chapter 3 for entering first graders are obvious. In Rohlen's (1974) ethnographic study of a bank, he details how new recruits are led into a large auditorium where senior officials and fellow employees greet them. They then hear speeches and songs and jointly take the company pledge. Parents are also invited and at one point a representative of the parents stands and makes a speech, thanking the company for hiring their children. It is both a solemn and festive occasion that is taken quite seriously by all involved. The commitment, after all, is great. The company will invest a great deal of time and money in the employee, providing intensive training as well as health and life insurance, retirement benefits, and oftentimes housing and even recreational facilities. It is also a great commitment for the employee who is expected to display loyalty to the company until retirement age (Abegglen and Stalk, Jr. [1985]).

After the ceremony, the new employees are carefully socialized into the company, being taught the company ideology during a rigorous three-month training session where they learn the history of the company, inspiring stories from past employees, memorize company songs, listen to speeches by management, and even endure a variety of grueling physical endurance tests. The purpose is to build strong camaraderie among members of the incoming cohort and also to develop in them a sense of company identity. Just as the school was thought of as "their" school, the company must now be thought of as "their" company. To this end, a great deal of effort is made. Not only do employees go through initial training sessions (the actual length of time varies from company to company), but also official ceremonies, sports days, and other social events are scheduled throughout the year to reinforce this sense of identity. Rohlen notes that at the bank he studied, there were thirteen official ceremonies and anywhere from six to twelve social events a year. As we noted in the previous chapter, this is not considered time wasted, but rather an important part of training. It is believed that a "unified body of employees" is necessary for a company to be successful (Iwata [1992]; Nishiyama and Matsumoto [1983]).

Thus, as in school, one is socialized in such a way as to develop a sense of identity with the organization and a sense of intimacy and dependence on one's group. Employees are constantly told of their company's history, replete with a full account of past struggles and successes, and encouraged to embrace the company and its goals as their own. In addition to ceremonies and social gatherings, most large companies have newsletters that attempt to encourage employees by recounting inspiring stories of past employees. Also, all employees are encouraged to contribute their own writing to the newsletters on a regular basis, thus reinforcing one's sense of belonging. Do all of these quite blatant attempts at socialization work, or are the employees sophisticated (and cynical) enough to view them as no more than self-serving company propaganda? There is reason to believe such socialization works, despite a relatively sophisticated and cynical workforce. The reason is that it is in the employee's best interest to accept and internalize the company's norms and values. Assuming that a new employee might very well spend his entire working life at this company, and is expected to both work and socialize with his coworkers and even put the needs of the company above the needs of his family, to *not* internalize the company's norms and values would make for a very long and unhappy life. In short, employees likely *want* to believe what the company tells them, since they have little choice but to act as if they really do believe it.

Another area where the similarity with school life is obvious is in the creation of small, cohesive groups. As in school, workers form small groups, and nearly all work is performed by the group rather than the individual. Furthermore, a worker is likely to stay in this group for many years, so good relations are essential. Thus, the company not only assigns work to the group, but also encourages group members to socialize together when they are not working. Rohlen (1989) writes:

Small groups are rarely just instrumental. Through informal socializing a bonding process occurs. Nowhere is this more notable than in company work groups and in the fact that weekend trips, after-work meals, and drinking parties are a regular aspect of the overall pattern, one encouraged by management. Eating, bathing, drinking, and sleeping together imitate in a limited way those most intimate of family activities. Patently, work groups are not families and these efforts should not be misunderstood as making them alike, yet the degree of attachment that does occur is the foundation of much social control. (47)

Lack of Alternatives

As discussed in the previous chapter, dependence arises not only through socialization, but also because of a lack of alternatives. This is no less true of the work environment than it was of the school environment. Just as it is difficult to change schools, it is also difficult to change jobs. This is especially true of white-collar jobs at large companies, but it is also true of employment in general. The reason it is especially true of white-collar positions at large companies is that they tend to hire once a year, and exclusively new college graduates. Transfers from other companies are not normally sought. After all, a transfer person has been socialized by another company and has learned different skills, work habits, and even ideologies. How would such a person fit in? Lacking the specific training program required by the company, he could not merely "take over" a position. And being older, he would be out of place attending the training session with the new recruits. Furthermore, such a person has already demonstrated a lack of loyalty to his previous employer, so it would be seen as risky to invest too much in him.

There is also the issue of pay. Most companies, large and small, tend to adhere to a seniority-based pay scale (Abegglen and Stalk, Jr. [1985]). Although there has often been talk of changing this system to reward merit, Dore, Bounine-Cabale, and Topiola (1989) note that statistical evidence shows that, if anything, seniority-based wages and promotions are even more central now than in the past, and the practice is spreading to smaller companies. In such a system, a person is rewarded for staying at the same company and punished for changing (by being made to begin again at the lowest position and salary). A comparison of job-changing in Japan and the United States found that although most Americans who change jobs do so to accept a better job elsewhere, Japanese who change jobs either remain at the same level or accept a lower-level job (Hechter and Kanazawa [1993]).

Although one might think that a system that promotes lifetime employment and seniority-based promotions and raises might not be able to effectively sanction inappropriate behavior, this is not the case. First, it is important to note that while everyone in a company can expect to be promoted, merit is also rewarded. After all, only a small number of any given cohort can become a section chief or manager. Thus, management does have the ability to threaten and sanction inappropriate behavior. However, the more important monitoring and sanctioning comes from one's coworkers rather than from management. Since work is often given to a group, and the group is evaluated by how well it performs the task, all members of the group suffer if one person fails to do his or her share. This places a great deal of peer pressure on all group members to contribute equally. The person who lets down the group will have to endure a negative relationship with his or her coworkers, a situation that is very uncomfortable given the amount of time everyone spends together.

Normative Obligations

Since levels of dependence are high, nurtured through socialization practices and reinforced through a hiring and salary system that rewards loyalty, so are normative obligations. Thus, companies often have strict and specific rules governing dress, behavior, and so on. The rules are contained in new employee handbooks, and they contain such regulations as governing where an employee can eat lunch, which elevators and bathrooms he or she can use, and oftentimes rules forbidding socializing with customers or bringing personal belongings to work. There are even long explanations of which phrases to use when speaking to customers and how to position one's hands and feet while speaking (Mouer and Sugimoto [1986]).

Of course, there are informal types of normative expectations associated with membership in any group, but they are especially high with work groups, where dependence is so high. A somewhat extreme example of these types of informal rules is the painted footprints along a walkway at a Toshiba factory with a sign telling employees how long it should take them to walk from one end to the other (Rohlen [1989]). A more common example is the social pressure to make many personal sacrifices for the good of the company, even when it means putting the company ahead of one's family. Also, there is the expectation that employees will participate in company social events, socialize after hours with coworkers, and either refuse to take a vacation or vacation with coworkers.

It is interesting to note that Japanese workers, despite their reputation, do not work an unusually long day nor are they particularly productive (as measured by real GDP divided by the number of employed persons). See Tables 4.1 and 4.2 for a cross-national comparison of these statistics.

TABLE 4.1   A Comparison of Annual Working Hours, 1995

Country	Total Annual Working Hours[a]	Overtime	Annual Holidays
Germany	1,550	88	145
France	1,680	—[b]	138
U.K.	1,943	198	136
Japan	1,975	152	125
United States	1,986	234	132

[a]Total working hours includes overtime.
[b]Separate overtime hours not available for France.
SOURCE: Japanese Ministry of Labor (1996).

TABLE 4.2   A Comparison of Labor Productivity, 1994

Country	Productivity
United States	136
France	130
Germany	124
Canada	112
U.K.	104
Japan	100
Sweden	100
South Korea	66

NOTE: International comparison is computed at purchasing power parity. Figures for Germany are for former West Germany.
SOURCE: Japan Productivity Center for Socioeconomic Development, as reported in the *Japan Almanac* (1998).

As can be seen in Table 4.1, Japanese workers work, on average, 1,975 hours annually (or about 247 eight-hour workdays a year). Although this figure is significantly higher than Germany and France, it is relatively comparable to the U.K. and the United States. Results from Table 4.2 are even more surprising. In terms of productivity (gross domestic product divided by the number of workers), the United States has the most productive workforce, followed by France and then Germany. Japan does not fare well in this international comparison, only outperforming South Korea. This is not meant to belittle the economic accomplishments of the Japanese workforce. It merely illustrates that although Japanese workers spend a great deal of time at work or with their coworkers, much of the time is dedicated to extracurricular activities. This is not to imply that the time is wasted. Again, from management's perspective, time spent reinforcing company ideology, socializing with coworkers, or attending weekend retreats is time well spent since it contributes to the cohesiveness of the group and increases a worker's sense of group identity and loyalty, all of which ultimately pay dividends.

Visibility, Monitoring, and Sanctioning

Dependence, then, works much the same way in the work environment as it does in the school environment. What about visibility? Again, the parallels are obvious. Since much time is spent working in groups and since evenings are often also spent with one's coworkers, there is little privacy. Individual work assignments, like individual offices, are not nearly as common in Japan as they are in the United States. Groups, not individuals, are given most tasks, and offices are typically large rooms with many desks, so that each person, even the section chiefs and managers, are under the watchful eye of everyone else, as illustrated by the cover photograph (Woronoff [1983]). Only 17 percent of Americans work in this type of "clerical pool" work environment. Mouer and Sugimoto (1986) characterize this work environment this way:

> Once employed, individuals are placed in a work situation conducive to group pressures and group policing. White-collar employees are not given private rooms or even partitioned workspace. Rather, under the *obeya* (large stable) system, they are required to work under the watchful eyes of their workmates. . . . Rather than being given initiative, workers are often prodded to work harder, with supervisors constantly circulating and looking over their shoulders. (252–253)

Beyond the immediate work environment, as was mentioned above, larger companies often provide free or subsidized housing for its employees. These facilities are particularly appealing for younger, single employees since they do not require large accommodations and they are not yet making a large salary (Rohlen [1974]). Of course, living under such arrangements provides the highest level of visibility, and for the group most in need of supervision. Employees are encouraged to spend their off hours at the housing establishment, either contributing to its upkeep or participating in exercise programs or social events with other employees. Dating is discouraged and, of course, employees are not permitted to bring people of the opposite sex back to their rooms. Thus, as with so many of these social arrangements, there is a give and take. The employer provides a great many social benefits to the employee, and the employee reciprocates by following a variety of normative obligations. Both parties incur a cost, but both parties benefit, as does social order as a whole.

When employees get older and marry, they often move into their own house or apartment (sometimes through a loan from the company). At this point, of course, visibility is decreased, but with little concern. It is well known that all forms of social deviance, especially criminal behavior, decrease markedly after about age twenty-five, especially for people who are married (Sampson and Laub [1990]; Steffensmeier et al. [1989]). Anyway, as discussed earlier, even though employees might no longer be living in company housing, they still spend the majority of their time, both during and after work, with their coworkers, so visibility continues well into the evening.

What about workers who do not work for large companies, or women who are out of the workforce? In general, workers at smaller companies are less dependent on their jobs. Smaller companies provide fewer benefits and less job security, and workers have greater job mobility than their counterparts at large companies. This does not mean, however, that these workers feel no sense of dependence. Changing jobs is still relatively difficult, and the chances of an upward change are very slim. Also, as mentioned earlier, many of the managerial techniques begun at larger companies have now trickled down to smaller ones, so it is not unusual to see smaller companies encouraging social activities and basing salaries on seniority (Dore, Bounine-Cabale, and Topiola [1989]). Nevertheless, these workers tend to be less dependent on their employers than are employees at large companies.

However, in terms of visibility, even workers in small companies live high visibility lives. General patterns of working in small groups, sharing work spaces, and socializing together afterward have become ubiquitous characteristics of the Japanese workforce (Tasker [1989]). Moreover, as with school life, employees at all levels spend so much time with their coworkers, either at work or socializing together after work, they have little time or opportunity to pursue a nonconventional lifestyle.

As briefly mentioned in the previous chapter, women are typically excluded from most career-track jobs. Women are often hired to temporary positions and are expected to quit when they marry (Brinton [1993]). Indeed, it has been argued that the main reason Japanese companies hire so many temporary female workers, often for jobs that require them to do little else than smile and greet customers, is to provide a pool of available women for the male employees to meet and marry (Alletzhauser [1990]). There have even been reports of large companies keeping photo albums of their female employees so that the male employees can look through and select someone they want to meet. This, of course, provides a very practical solution to an otherwise difficult problem. With men spending all of their time at work or in the company of coworkers, they have no time to actively search for a spouse. By hiring a large number of young, single females, the company can provide their single male employees with potential mates and can also exercise some control over the types of women their male employees meet and eventually marry.

Even if a female employee wanted to continue working after marriage, much of the social structure is constructed in such a way as to discourage that option (Brinton [1993]). First, as mentioned above, companies typically hire women only in temporary positions as support staff. Females do not receive the types of training that male employees do, nor are they promoted along with their male counterparts. Second, even if a woman wanted to remain with a company after marriage, there are many incentives for her to quit. Many companies offer a type of severance pay to women to encourage them to quit after a certain number of years of employment, and that amount is often doubled or even tripled if the woman marries within three months of quitting her job. Of course, the reason is to encourage women to quit at the time of their marriage. Also, once a woman has a child, it is very difficult to continue working because of a lack of child care services, maternity leave, and a variety of other institutional barriers (see Kodera [1994]; Brinton [1993, 1989]). This topic will discussed in greater depth in Chapter 5.

Returning to the issue of behavioral conformity based on group dependence and visibility, the above discussion would imply that women are far less dependent on jobs (as well as school) than men, and once they are married and out of the workforce, women are also far less visible. This is true. However, there are two important points to keep in mind when discussing overall social order. First, the types of nonconventional behavior participated in by women tend to have less of a direct impact on social order than the types of nonconventional behavior participated in by men. Or put more simply, men require social control more than women in order for a society to maintain high social order. For example, men are far more likely than women to participate in violent or aggressive behavior (South and Messner [1987]; Stark [1998]). Studies of deviant behavior suggest that men are likely to behave in socially destructive ways when social control mechanisms break down, whereas women are more likely to participate in self-destructive behavior (Schur [1983]). Thus, male deviant behavior includes thrill-seeking behavior such as speeding, taking drugs, and so on, and aggressive behavior such as violent crimes. Female deviant behavior, on the other hand, tends to disproportionately involve diet-related problems, abuse of prescriptive drugs, joining religious cults, or suffering from different types of psychological problems, most of which tend to be self-destructive. Although such self-destructive behavior is not desirable in any society, it has less of a direct impact on typical measures of social order than male deviant behavior.

Furthermore, as was mentioned with males, all forms of deviant behavior decrease by the time a person is in his or her mid-twenties. The majority of women in Japan work until this age. Indeed, among Japanese workers under the age of twenty-five, approximately 48 percent are female (*Japan Almanac* [1998]). Therefore, there are social control mechanisms at work during the period when females are most likely to engage in nonconventional behavior.

One more aspect of the Japanese social system should be discussed in relation to increased visibility among all of its citizens. There is a national family register system *(koseki)* that records detailed information about a person and his or her family. Not only does the *koseki* contain normal vital statistics such as births and deaths for all family members going back many generations, but also records information regarding marriages, divorces, arrests, cause of deaths of relatives, and so on. Also, a complete list of past addresses are available (through a part of the *koseki* called the *honseki*) so that much information about the individual can be gleaned (Taylor [1983]). Although these records are not public, it is not unusual for perspective employers or spouses to ask to see a person's family register before any decisions are made. It is, therefore, very difficult to hide one's past or the past of one's relatives.

Conclusion

Murakami and Rohlen (1992) and Kumon (1992) describe Japanese society, and especially the Japanese workforce, as a complex web of personal relationships and networks that run through all levels of society. Although some are close, tight-knit groups, and others are merely loose-knit connections, they all operate similarly in terms of a hierarchical and systematic set of generalized exchanges. In such a system, one must at times subjugate one's own personal interests and desires for the good of the group. In exchange for this sacrifice, one can expect a variety of future rewards. This type of system, based on long-term generalized exchanges rather than short-term reciprocity, maintains its legitimacy only as long as it is able to fulfill its long-term obligations to its members. It cannot be maintained merely through a cultural legacy of collectivist thinking. The only way it can work, then, is in a society where relationships are long-term (i.e., it is difficult to change group affiliations) and failure to meet social obligations are not tolerated (i.e., there is effective monitoring and sanctioning). Thus, in order to maintain this web of social networks and associations, a unique social structural system exists in Japan.

In this chapter, we have discussed how the Japanese employment system is geared toward supporting this type of long-term generalized exchange. The system is set up to penalize workers who change jobs, and a high visibility environment, coupled with high dependence on the group, makes monitoring and sanctioning easy and effective. Although the expressed reason for such a system is not to produce and maintain social order, but rather to produce and maintain a long-term social exchange system that is able to achieve group goals and fulfill future obligations to its members, it unintentionally also leads to high social order. In other words, social order in Japan is not primarily maintained through the enactment of laws, the presence of police, the actions of politicians, or even the internalization of prosocial morals and values; rather, it is the by-product of a web of social networks and small groups, each maintaining order in pursuit of its own long-term objectives. In this regard, education and employment are the social institutions most responsible for order.

We will next turn our attention to family life in Japan, and consider a somewhat different structural characteristic that also contributes to high social order.

5

The Family

The previous chapter noted the strong gender-based division of labor that exists in Japan. In this chapter we will elaborate on Japan's gender-based division of labor, discuss typical family patterns, especially for females, and then discuss how these patterns are relevant to our discussion of social order. The purpose is not to provide a detailed discussion of Japanese family patterns (many excellent books exist that discuss the *ie,* Japan's traditional family structure and its impact on modern society—see, for example, Murakami, Kumon, and Sato [1979]). Nor will we attempt to provide a detailed discussion of gender roles or gender discrimination (Brinton [1993] provides an excellent discussion of this topic). Our purpose, instead, is to provide an overview of current family patterns and assess how a gender-based division of labor impacts social order.

Division of Labor

Despite modernization patterns similar to those in the West (i.e., the collapse of a feudal society followed by rapid urbanization and industrialization), Japan remains more traditional in terms of a gender-based division of labor than most other modern, industrialized societies. There are probably two reasons for this. First, traditional gender roles are still encouraged as part of the general socialization process, and many Japanese, both males and females, have adopted these social values. Second, the structure of modern Japanese society promotes a gender-based division of labor by effectively excluding females from long-term labor-force participation.

In terms of the first reason, recall that socialization in Japan is far more uniform and systematic than it is in the United States or in many other countries. This is owing largely to the uniformity and importance of the formal education system. The education system not only promotes a specific curriculum that includes moral education, but also has a complex track system that guides students onto different career trajectories (see Tsukahara, Noro, and Kobayashi [1990]; Fujita [1985]). Although females are permitted to follow a university preparatory track, they do not receive the same encouragement, either from their schools or from their families, as male students. Some telling statistics are presented by Brinton (1993) concerning mothers' aspirations for their sons' and daughters' education as well as their attitudes toward socializing their children. These statistics are reproduced in Table 5.1. Clearly, Japanese mothers show the greatest disparity between educational aspirations for their sons and those for their daughters. Also, Japan has the highest percentage of mothers who believe boys and girls ought to be socialized differently.

Despite these statistics, it would be unfair to merely characterize Japanese mothers as "traditional." As mentioned in Chapter 3, patterns of socialization take into account the current social structure. Japanese mothers know perfectly well how difficult it is for females to succeed in the Japanese labor market. Indeed, female university graduates are actually *less* likely to be hired by a major corporation than are female high school graduates (Brinton [1993]). The reason is simple. Females are expected to marry and quit at about age twenty-five. University graduates are not only older than high school graduates, and therefore close to "retirement" age, they are also less content to accept a lower-level temporary position. Clearly, Japanese mothers are aware of this situation. If the situation were different and there were ample career opportunities for women, more mothers would likely encourage their daughters to go to college.

In a sense, Japan is caught in a system that is self-perpetuating. The labor market contains a gender bias, which leads to gender-biased socialization patterns. These socialization patterns then reinforce the structure of the labor market. It is difficult to break this pattern. Although it is possible to change the socialization process and create a generation of women able to spearhead a successful feminist movement, it is more common for structural conditions to change, thus allowing women entry into the labor force. Such a change might be occurring now, although it is too early to be certain. The Japanese population is currently declining because of a low birthrate. When the baby boomers retire in the next ten or so years, there will be a labor shortage. Such a shortage might create a situation where women are able to gain increased access into the labor market.

Nevertheless, the current situation in Japan is one where traditional gender roles persist. Other cross-national surveys consistently show that Japan is among the most traditional countries in terms of attitudes

TABLE 5.1   Mothers' Attitudes Toward Their Sons and Daughters

Country	*Aspire to University Education for:* Sons (%)	Daughters (%)	*Believe Boys and Girls Should Be Socialized Differently (%)*
Japan	73.0	27.7	62.6
South Korea	88.3	81.2	—
Sweden	87.3	84.5	6.0
United States	68.9	65.8	31.3
Philippines	48.1	44.1	28.1
West Germany	31.1	30.8	19.9
England	19.6	14.3	20.1

SOURCE: Office of the Prime Minister, Japan (1982); Korea Survey by Gallup (1987 [as reported by Brinton 1993]).

toward gender roles. Table 5.2 presents additional examples of this. The first column reports reactions to the statement that "being a housewife is just as fulfilling as working for pay." The lower the mean response, the more traditional the response (i.e., the greater the amount of agreement with the statement). Japanese respondents were more likely to agree with that statement than were respondents from other countries. The second column reports reactions to the statement that "what most women really want is a home and child." Again, Japanese respondents generally agreed with that statement, the only country showing stronger agreement being South Korea. Finally, the third column displays reaction to the statement that when jobs are scarce, men have more of a right to jobs than women. Again, Japanese respondents generally agreed with that statement, ranking second only to South Korea.

An interesting side note concerning this table is that most countries cannot be accurately characterized as either traditional or nontraditional, vis-à-vis other industrialized countries. For example, the United States is quite traditional in its attitudes toward housework being fulfilling, but relatively nontraditional concerning the allocation of scarce jobs. However, both Japan and South Korea are consistently traditional in their attitudes toward gender roles, while the country that is most consistently nontraditional is Denmark.

Further evidence of Japan's traditional attitudes toward gender roles comes from a 1995 national survey. Table 5.3 presents results from that survey, broken down by sex. The first section asked people to respond to the statement that women are better than men at housework and raising children. As can be seen, a majority of both men and women agreed with that statement. About 78 percent of the men agreed, and about 67 percent

TABLE 5.2   Attitudes Toward Traditional Gender Roles

Country	Housewife Fulfilling[a]	Woman Wants Home and Child[a]	Scarce Jobs Go to Men[b]
Japan	2.01	2.02	1.92
South Korea	2.05	1.94	1.86
United States	2.07	2.36	2.47
Belgium	2.12	2.25	2.14
Canada	2.14	2.57	2.56
Sweden	2.20	—	2.80
France	2.27	2.14	2.26
Spain	2.30	2.39	2.34
U.K.	2.34	2.51	2.24
Netherlands	2.34	2.65	2.45
Denmark	2.34	2.87	2.75
West Germany	2.41	2.49	2.28
Italy	2.42	2.18	2.08

[a]Scale of 1–4, the lower number indicates agreement.
[b]Scale of 1–3, the lower number indicates agreement.
SOURCE: World Values Survey (1991).

of the women agreed. The second part of the table states that housework is very important to society. The response is similar, with a majority of both men and women agreeing with the statement.

Thus, there appears to be widespread acceptance of traditional gender roles. Although, as mentioned above, this might reflect an attempt to rationalize social reality, it is also important to note that many women prefer this arrangement. A point often lost when Westerners observe gender issues is that housewives in Japan have considerable autonomy and power. With husbands spending little time at home, wives enjoy considerable freedom and control over most family affairs. It is common for the husband to turn over his paycheck to his wife, who then allocates money as she deems appropriate (Watanabe [1995]). Thus women make most financial decisions for a family. They also, of course, are in charge of raising the children and therefore make all decisions concerning the child's education. Thus, housewives in Japan enjoy a relatively high degree of power and status.

It is also important to note that the male work environment in Japan is not necessarily attractive. Sumiko Iwao (1995) offers the following observation:

Once it was women who were chained, responsible for family and household, while men were free to pursue power, wealth, and adventure outside

TABLE 5.3   Japanese Attitudes Toward a Gender-Based Division of Labor

	Percent Agree	Percent Disagree
Women Are Better than Men at		
Housework and Raising Children:		
Male	78.2	21.8
Female	67.4	32.6
A Housewife's Work Is Very		
Important to Society:		
Male	70.4	29.6
Female	62.7	37.3

SOURCE: Japanese Social Stratification and Mobility (SSM) Survey (1995).

the home. But now men have become increasingly chained to the institutions they have set up, with their commitment to long-term employment and the promotional ladder rigged to seniority. Their wives, on the other hand, have been set free by the development of home appliances and other conveniences, and now their ability and energy is being absorbed by a waiting labor market and a broad range of culturally enriching activities. Not only can they work outside the home, but they have great freedom to decide how, where, and under what terms they will work. The female side of society has become extremely diversified, while the male side, trapped by inertia and peer pressure, has grown more homogeneous. (180)

Iwao goes on to suggest that society would be better served if, rather than women being allowed to assume positions in the labor market comparable to men, men were allowed to pursue positions comparable to women.

The second reason stated above for the continuation of a traditional gender-based division of labor in Japan is the structure of modern Japanese society, which perpetuates traditional gender roles. It was already stated that the education system tends to encourage male students, more so than female students, to prepare for college entrance exams. The result is a bifurcated higher education system. Half of the females who go to college enter two-year junior colleges and the other half enter universities. However, of the males who enter college, over 90 percent enter universities (*Japan Almanac* [1998]).

Many companies promote the same type of bifurcated system, with the existence of male and female employment tracks. This was already discussed briefly in the previous chapter. Although the position of women in the workforce has improved somewhat since Rodney Clark, in his influential 1979 book on Japanese companies, baldly declared that "Japanese companies do not promote women," much still remains the same. Companies still typically hire women only in temporary positions as support staff, and these women do not receive benefits or training comparable to male employees. Although few companies have explicit rules that mandate retirement upon marriage, that is still the expected norm. And as we have noted throughout this book, norm expectations are usually adhered to in Japan. In a 1988 survey conducted by the Japanese Ministry of Labor, it was found that only 13.5 percent of married female workers who were in their forties had worked continuously since they were in their twenties (Brinton [1993]). Besides, there are financial incentives to quit. As noted in Chapter 4, women are often given lump sums of money in the form of severance pay if they marry within three months of quitting their jobs. There are also significant tax benefits that encourage married women to either not work at all or work at part-time jobs. If a spouse earns less than 1,000,000 yen (approximately $9,000 at the current exchange rate), her earnings are tax free. However, if she earns more than that, the tax rate for the couple increases dramatically.

Reforming this gender-based tracking system has proven difficult and has led to a chicken or egg debate. Employers note that training procedures for new employees involve a sizable commitment of company resources. For male employees who will remain with the company for many years, this commitment makes sense. However, since many females choose to quit their jobs either when they marry or when they have their first child, it makes little sense for companies to commit the same amount of time and money to training female employees as they do male employees. Thus, employers claim they cannot change the system unless attitudes among females change so that they can feel confident that their investment will not be wasted. Although this sounds reasonable, a recent survey of female employees revealed that 77 percent believed their company will request that they resign upon the birth of their first child (Watanabe [1995]). Furthermore, Brinton (1993) reports that many young women are advised to tell their prospective employers that they plan to quit upon marriage since it increases their chances of being hired. This appears to contradict the claim by employers that they are reluctant to invest in women because they might quit. If this were really the case, they would be looking for career-oriented women who did not plan to quit upon marriage rather than women who plan to quit. This appears, instead, to support the claims made earlier that employers are primarily interested in hiring potential brides for their male employees.

Family Patterns

Although there are obviously exceptions, the typical modern Japanese family develops the following way. Both males and females, after either graduating high school or college, enter the labor market. Males typically are hired to long-term jobs while females are hired to short-term jobs. During this time, males and females often continue living with their parents. There are two reasons for this. First, housing is very expensive in Japan, so living at home makes good economic sense. Second, companies that do not provide housing encourage single employees to live with their parents since they believe they will be less likely to get into trouble (i.e., living at home ensures a high visibility environment where parents can monitor and sanction their child's inappropriate behavior). In fact, many companies make it a policy not to hire people who live alone, especially females who live alone (Brinton [1993]). By their mid- to late twenties, the overwhelming majority of people marry. For males, the average age of marriage is twenty-nine and for females it is twenty-six (Iwao [1995]). As discussed above, either upon marriage or upon the birth of a child, the overwhelmingly percentage of females quit their jobs. They then dedicate themselves to managing family affairs and raising the children. When the children reach high school or college age, about 70 percent of the women return to the labor force, again working at part-time or temporary jobs (Brinton [1993]).

Japan has a birthrate of 1.5, meaning couples have, on average, one and a half children. This is among the lowest birthrates in the world (despite recent efforts by the Japanese government to encourage couples to have more children). Therefore, the typical family has only one or two children, and mothers spend a great deal of time and energy on child care, especially as it involves education. Since men are usually required to spend long hours at their place of employment and then socialize afterward with coworkers, they are largely uninvolved in household decision making or the children's education.

Thus, there are clear roles designated for men and women, and the low incidence of divorce in Japan reflects the fact that as long as husbands and wives fulfill their expected roles, the marriage will continue. Iwao (1995) summarizes this arrangement by the following statement: "Women who spend little time with their husbands, communicate with them even less, and share with them only a long-term trust that the other person will always be there will, after twenty or thirty years of marriage, establish independent life-styles totally suited to their respective needs" (190). The idea of divorcing because the couple is not in love or because their lives have grown apart is uncommon in Japan. These are rarely a couple's expectations when entering a marriage. Expectations with marriage, as with other social institutions in Japan, are for all participants to act responsibly and to conform to social norms. Of course, as in any country, people marry for a variety of reasons and hold a variety of expectations for their marriage. However, the pattern described above is still extremely common in Japan, and divorce is relatively rare.

Relationship to Social Control

The type of traditional family pattern and gender-based division of labor described above, although admittedly restrictive, appears to contribute to the high level of social order in Japan. As with other aspects of life in Japan, there is a price to pay for increased social order, and that price usually entails behavioral restrictions on the individual. Without condoning such restrictions, it is important to understand the relationship of behavioral restrictions to overall social order. In past chapters we observed how the education and employment systems restrict individual choice and in so doing maintain high levels of social control and ultimately high levels of social order. Traditional family and gender patterns appear to do the same.

Promoting a traditional gender-based division of labor likely contributes to high levels of social order in several distinct ways. First, consider the low incidence of divorce in Japan. The majority of social science studies of divorce show that it has a strong negative impact on children. There is near unanimous agreement that children whose parents divorce have a variety of problems, including higher rates of delinquency, lower self-esteem, increased problems with interpersonal relationships, and so on (Amato [1993]; Wallerstein and Blakeslee [1989]). It is useful, in addition, to note that past research also suggests that the actual event of divorce is related to the more psychological issues of interpersonal relationships and self-esteem. Behavioral problems, such as delinquency, are more related to the decrease in parental supervision that usually accompanies a divorce.

Consistent with those observations, past research by criminologists and criminological sociologists show that parental supervision is closely associated with rates of juvenile delinquency (Kornhauser [1978]; Sampson [1987]; Patterson and Dishion [1985]). This, of course, makes good intuitive sense. We have discussed throughout this book that social control is best maintained in high visibility environments where inappropriate behavior can be observed and sanctioned. Obviously, the absence of parents will greatly reduce the amount of control parents can exercise over a child's behavior. Divorced couples, along with single-parent households and even dual-earner households, are all family structures where there is less parental supervision than in households where one parent is always home. Japan not only has one of the lowest divorce rates of any modern industrialized country, but it also has the lowest rate of single-parent households. Whereas around 25 percent of all births in the United States are to unmarried women, only about 1 percent are to unmarried women in Japan (Jetro [1991]). Furthermore, Japan also has more multigenerational families than any other modern industrialized country

(Kamo [1990]). Of adults over the age of sixty, 70 percent live with their children, 20 percent live with their spouse, and only the remaining 10 percent live alone (Long [1987]). Thus, the high percentage of intact families and multigenerational families, as well as the high percentage of stay-at-home mothers, provides a family environment with high levels of adult and parental supervision. This, in turn, contributes to the relatively low rates of juvenile delinquency in Japan. This specific topic will be considered in greater detail in Chapter 6 when we discuss crime.

There is yet another way that a gender-based division of labor, or more specifically, gender discrimination in the workplace, contributes to high social order in Japan. It is a well-known fact that the overwhelming majority of criminals, especially those participating in violent crimes, are young males. Although we will go into more detail on this topic in the next chapter, suffice it to say that employed young males are far less likely to participate in criminal activities than are unemployed young males. By relegating females to temporary support staff who can be hired and fired as economic trends dictate, jobs and job security for young males can be maintained. Clearly, this practice that unfairly exploits the female workforce and assures high employment rates for young males has positive effects on social order. Compare this situation with the United States, which tends to discriminate against young people, especially young black males. Labor market statistics for 1998 provided by the U.S. Bureau of Labor Statistics show that although the overall U.S. unemployment rate is currently quite low (about 4.6 percent), it rises to 10.8 percent for people ages sixteen to twenty-four who are actively seeking employment. It is even higher, 11.2 percent, for male youths, and 24.8 percent for black youths (information for black males was not available, but since males tend to have higher unemployment rates than females, the actual unemployment rate for black males is likely higher than 25 percent).

Conclusion

As with other areas of Japanese society, attitudes toward traditional gender roles and the structure of the family provide an interesting contrast with other modern industrialized societies. Although it is tempting to characterize these differences in strictly negative terms, not because they are traditional, per se, but because they involve discriminatory practices, the topic is complex. The labor market not only discriminates against females, but it also discriminates against males who prefer not to dedicate their lives to their companies. In this sense, rather than characterizing the Japanese labor market as gender biased, it might be more accurate to describe it as monolithic in that its uniform structure restricts the lives of both males and females. Yet this structure, although it clearly constricts the individual, is not without its merits. Furthermore, these merits are recognized by a good many Japanese, as is evidenced by the surveys cited earlier that support traditional gender roles.

We have already discussed various topics where individuality and freedom of choice are sacrificed, not wholly voluntarily, because the social structure and social norms dictate such a sacrifice. Such sacrifices are not necessarily antithetical to one's own self-interests. Benefits from conforming to these normative expectations are twofold. First and most directly, the individual benefits by entering into a relationship characterized by long-term security and a high level of predictability. Indirectly, the individual benefits by increases in overall social order. The gender and family patterns discussed above appear to be yet another example of this type of exchange.

Of course, the above discussion is not meant to condone discriminatory hiring practices or suggest that the Japanese pattern is the only one capable of maintaining social order. There are many examples of countries that have nontraditional attitudes toward gender roles, nondiscriminatory hiring practices, and relatively high divorce rates that still maintain relatively high levels of social order, at least as measured by crime statistics. Social control can be produced in a variety of ways. Our purpose throughout this book is merely to describe how it is produced in Japan.

Finally, we note that quite recently there has been a rise in discipline problems in elementary and junior high school classes. Teachers report that their classrooms have "collapsed," meaning that disruptive behavior has increased to the point where normal classroom activities are affected. Although such behavior is still low compared to other countries, it is interesting to note that many Japanese social scientists blame recent changes in the family structure as the root cause. Specifically, recent increases in divorce, dual-income couples, and a decrease in multigenerational families have been blamed for this increase. Also, the low birthrate, resulting in families spoiling their only child, is being blamed for these problems. Whether these problems truly are related to recent changes in the family structure, and whether they will result in more serious disruptions to overall social order are clearly questions that social scientists will be addressing in years to come.

6

Crime

The relevance of understanding small-group social control mechanisms to the study of crime is obvious. Since behavior is so well controlled through informal social controls (e.g., monitoring and sanctioning) at the group level, and therefore behavioral conformity is high, crime rates are naturally low in Japan. Because social stigma is strong, and one's actions not only reflect on the person but also affect his or her group, the consequences of inappropriate behavior are severe. Thus, the price one pays for any type of deviant behavior, especially criminal deviant behavior, is very high. Indeed, the police have the luxury of taking a relatively leisurely approach to apprehending criminals, often waiting long periods of time for the accused to turn him or herself in. After all, since most people have some type of fixed group affiliation, it is very difficult to run and hide. It would involve leaving a fixed group and either living the life of a loner or trying to enter a new group, both of which are extremely difficult to do in Japan.

Before considering more systematically how this type of social structure inhibits crime, we first look more closely at some cross-national crime rates. Chapter 1 presented homicide rates for various countries. We now expand that table to consider a wider range of crimes, including robbery, assault, theft, and burglary. But before reviewing these statistics, a variety of definitions and caveats are necessary. Robbery is typically defined as forcibly taking something from someone (i.e., it involves a face-to-face encounter). Assault is defined as physically attacking someone with the intent of inflicting injury. Theft, which is sometimes referred to as larceny, involves stealing something from someone without a direct face-to-face threat of physical violence (e.g., shoplifting, picking pockets, stealing a bicycle, and so on). Note that this excludes car theft, which is kept as a separate statistic in most countries. Finally, burglary involves entering someone else's property with the intention of stealing something (Maguire, Pastore, and Flanagan [1993]).

These definitions are fairly straightforward, but comparing crime rates cross-nationally is anything but straightforward. There are variations in these definitions that produce variations in the statistics, such as distinguishing between major and minor assaults and thefts, or even differences in definitions of what constitutes a crime. Furthermore, crime statistics represent the number of crimes reported to the police. There are wide variations in the reporting of crimes from country to country. A country that has an ineffective police force will receive fewer reports since the citizens do not believe reporting will do any good. Thus, they will appear to have a lower crime rate than they actually have. More seriously, some crimes, such as rape, spouse abuse, and child abuse, are seriously underreported, and the degree to which they are underreported varies greatly from society to society. Thus, all cross-national comparisons should be viewed with some skepticism. Nevertheless, if treated carefully, they can provide a general picture of relative crime rates. In Table 6.1 we report crime rates, limiting our analysis to modern industrialized countries and reporting only crimes that have relatively uniform definitions and reporting patterns.

Caveats aside, it seems clear that in general the United States has a very high crime rate vis-à-vis other modern industrialized countries, particularly with regard to homicide and robbery. It is even clearer that Japan enjoys a uniquely low crime rate. In this table, we included crime statistics from the Republic of Korea and the Philippines, since these two countries are also part of Far East Asia and are geographically close to Japan. (Unfortunately, reliable crime data are not yet available from China.) As can be seen, Japan's crime rate is uniquely low, even when compared to its Asian neighbors. Although both neighbors report relatively low robbery rates, they are still significantly higher than in Japan. More important, homicide rates tend to be the most accurate crime statistic. Although other categories, such as robbery, tend to be greatly underreported (since objects stolen are sometimes of little value, and the victim often feels reporting the robbery to the police will not do any good), homicides are almost always reported (although obviously not by the victim). Therefore, they are probably the best crime statistic to compare cross-nationally. As can be seen, Korea and the Philippines both report very high homicide rates, while Japan reports the lowest.

Although the causes of crime might very well differ from country to country and from crime to crime, the distinctively low crime rate in Japan is likely linked to elements of the social structure that we have been describing in this book. We will now consider this more in depth by focusing first on general theories of crime and then on relevant aspects of the Japanese social structure.

TABLE 6.1   Cross-National Crime Rates per 100,000 Population

Country	Homicide	Robbery	Assault	Theft	Burglary
Republic of Korea	10.1	10.3	—	—	—
Philippines	9.4	13.7	—	—	—
United States	9.0	237.5	427.1	3613.7	1040.9
Italy	5.3	52.4	36.5	2330.9	—
Denmark	5.1	93.8	189.8	3963.1	2043.0
Australia	4.9	80.1	—	—	2130.0
Germany	3.9	48.6	—	—	—
Austria	3.5	30.4	419.2	1582.3	1122.7
Belgium	3.4	14.4	330.6	2733.0	1534.3
Switzerland	3.1	27.9	51.6	2793.6	950.2
Scotland	2.2	103.2	115.3	4641.8	1722.3
Canada	2.0	98.8	771.4	3430.4	1326.2
U.K.	1.4	116.2	408.9	4863.6	2445.4
Japan	1.4	2.2	19.3	1049.8	198.5

SOURCE: United Nations World Crime Survey (1995).

Theories of Crime

Broadly speaking, we can conceive of criminological theories as falling into four categories: structural theories, learning theories, control theories, and theories of deterrence. Although these theories cover a wide range of social issues and behavior, they are all either directly or indirectly related to issues raised in this book. It is therefore useful to review all four areas to gain a more complete understanding of why crime rates are so low in Japan.

Structural Theories

Structural theories emphasize characteristics of society that either promote criminal behavior (as well as other forms of deviant behavior), or fail to discourage such behavior. Often the focus is on the relationship between increased social complexities and increased crime (see Laub [1983]; Bursik [1988]; Sampson [1987, 1988]; Sampson and Groves [1989]). As societies become more urban, traditional means of social control become less effective. In smaller, more traditional communities, behavior is more easily controlled since everyone knows everyone else, and a person's role in the community, as well as the norms governing appropriate behavior, are known by all. However, in urban areas, characterized by more complex living arrangements and increased community heterogeneity, social control mechanisms, as well as knowledge of social norms, break down. The breakdown in social control mechanisms is often called "social disorganization," while the breakdown in knowledge of social norms is called "anomie."

More concretely, in small towns local agents of socialization (e.g., family, church, neighborhood, and community leaders) tend to have a fair amount of influence on everyone. In a sense, small-town life is much like group life in Japan. Everyone knows everyone else, so people live in high visibility environments. And since, under such conditions, a person's reputation is of great importance, the consequences of inappropriate behavior can be severe (see Braithwaite [1989] for an excellent discussion of the importance of protecting one's reputation in Japan). However, in large cities where the sheer size of the population increases an individual's anonymity and transportation systems make it easy to move quickly and easily from one place to another, the power of the community to regulate behavior is largely undermined. Cities afford greater individual freedom, but along with that freedom comes potentially dangerous unregulated behavior.

There are also other structural characteristics of cities that influence crime rates. Many neighborhoods have high levels of residential mobility. That is, people move in and out of neighborhoods frequently. Under such conditions, community support groups are less likely to develop and it becomes more difficult to spot strangers in the neighborhood. Also, since it is increasingly common in many cities in many modern industrialized countries for both parents to work, there is less parental supervision of children. This all leads to an increased likelihood of crime in many urban areas.

A second strain of structural theories focuses less on the characteristics of neighborhoods and more on the macro characteristics of a society. Of particular importance is the relationship between crime rates and unemployment rates. A variety of studies have shown that crime rates tend to be sensitive to economic trends and generally increase as unemployment rates increase (Grant and Martinez [1997]; Sampson [1987]).

In general, then, structural theories have much in common with issues raised in this book. Low crime (i.e., high social order) is closely related to the degree to which informal social control networks are able to regulate behavior. Restated using theoretical concepts employed in this book, structural theorists claim that a main reason crime is lower in rural than in urban areas is that rural areas are characterized by high visibility, where social agents are able to monitor and sanction inappropriate behavior, and where the consequences of deviant behavior are more severe.

Learning Theories

Learning theorists note that all human behavior, whether normative or deviant, is learned. Therefore, criminal behavior should be approached in much the same way any other behavior is studied. In general, these theories focus on social interaction, especially within intimate groups (e.g., close friends and family) (Sutherland [1947]; Burgess and Akers [1966]; Akers [1985]; Matsueda and Heimer [1987]). Through these associations people learn not only the actual behavior, but also supporting attitudes, values, and rationalizations. For example, people typically begin using illegal drugs when they become friends with drug users. From these friends they not only learn the behavior (how to purchase and use the drug), but also supporting attitudes such as the rejection of mainstream condemnation of drug use.

In general, there are two ways people learn behavior: by modeling (copying others) and by operant conditioning (having one's behavior shaped through a series of rewards and punishments). Studies focusing on modeling claim that the more time a person spends around criminals and deviants and the more he or she admires and respects these people, the more likely he or she is to begin copying their behavior (Sutherland [1947]; Cressey [1960]; Glaser [1956]). Studies focusing on operant conditioning claim that in order to understand criminal and deviant behavior, it is necessary to focus on the rewards and punishments associated with it (Akers et al. [1979]; Akers [1985]). Put more simply, learning theories focus on basic socialization practices, since socialization involves watching and copying friends and family (modeling), and learning appropriate behavior by being rewarded and punished by family and friends (operant conditioning).

A variant of learning theory, which is closely related to issues discussed in this book, is subculture theory. Although learning theorists emphasize the need to understand criminal and deviant behavior as learned human behavior, subculture theorists emphasize that most behavior is not only learned, but actually conforming in nature. The difference between deviant and normative behavior is not that one person accepts social norms and the other rejects them; rather, the difference involves conforming to different sets of social norms (Banfield [1968]; Wolfgang and Ferracuti [1967]). Criminals and deviants often live in social environments where conforming to social norms involves participating in criminal or deviant behavior. An obvious example would be members of a street gang. Clearly, gang members are deviants, and often participate in criminal activities. Yet it would be misleading to classify them as nonconformists. If anything, gang members tend to live in an environment that requires more behavioral conformity and rule following than non–gang members. Thus, like learning theorists, subculture theorists emphasize the situational nature of deviant behavior and the natural learning processes that lead normal people to participate in criminal activities.

Control Theories

Control theorists approach the study of crime and deviance from a very different angle. They begin by noting that much deviant behavior is intrinsically rewarding. Elaborate theories are not necessary to explain why someone steals money or takes drugs. People steal money because it is of value, and they take drugs because it is pleasurable. Although not all criminal and deviant behavior is directly rewarding in this way, much of it is, and even those acts that are not can be rewarding simply because they *are* deviant. There is a certain intrinsic pleasure associated with breaking social norms. Therefore, for the control theorist the interesting question is not why 5 to 10 percent of a population in any given country participates in criminal or deviant behavior, but rather why 90 percent do not (Hirschi [1969]; Wiatrowski, Griswold, and Roberts [1981]; Sampson and Laub [1990]; Cernkovich and Giordano [1992]).

The answer to this question was most clearly presented by Hirschi (1969), who suggested four factors that tend to inhibit a person's natural desire to commit a deviant act (Hirschi refers to these as four social bonds). They are attachments, investments, involvement, and beliefs. "Attachments" refers to interpersonal relationships. The more one is involved in strong relationships with others (obviously these others must be nondeviants), the less likely one is to commit a criminal or deviant act for fear of injuring that relationship. In support of this, control theorists note that people with strong family ties tend to follow social norms, and virtually all forms of criminal and deviant behavior decline when a person marries or has children (Liska [1987]; Kornhauser [1978]). "Investments" refers to the degree to which a person is invested in conventional society, or more simply, what a person stands to lose if caught committing a criminal act. For example, a person who has a good job is more strongly invested in conventional society than a person who is unemployed. Similarly, a college graduate is more strongly invested than a high school dropout. It would make little sense for a bank manager with a good salary to rob a convenience store. He or she has too much to lose.

The third social bond is involvement. "Involvement" merely refers to the amount of time a person spends in conventional activities. Obviously, the busier a person is, the less likely it is that he or she will be involved in criminal or deviant acts, merely because of a lack of time. This is similar to the old adage "idle hands are the devil's workshop." Finally, "beliefs" refers to the socialization process, and specifically to the internalization of social norms and values. People are able to exhibit self-control because they believe that it is wrong to break laws or commit other deviant acts.

In sum, control theorists believe that people are naturally inclined to commit a variety of criminal or deviant acts, but exhibit self-control. The reason they exhibit self-control is that they have ties to conventional society. The ties are in the form of attachments, investments, involvement, and beliefs. The stronger these ties, the less likely they are to engage in nonconventional behavior, since they have a stake in conventional society. Or put more in terms of our theoretical perspective, ties to conventional society constitute an increase in dependence, as well as an increased likelihood of being surrounded by people who will sanction inappropriate behavior.

Theories of Deterrence

Deterrence is the means by which criminal justice systems attempt to inhibit criminal behavior (i.e., the primary *formal* social control mechanism used in most societies). It works on the basic assumption that if there is a serious price to be paid for criminal behavior (e.g., a jail sentence, monetary fine, and so on), people will think twice about breaking the law. In other words, the goal of deterrence is to make the potential cost of committing a criminal act higher than the potential reward. Or put more simply, the criminal justice system attempts to scare people into compliance with society's rules. This concept has a long history, and can be traced back to Plato, who said "the man who is punished, and the man who sees him punished, may be deterred from doing wrong again" (as quoted in Stark [1998]). This theoretical perspective obviously differs from the others. The other theories are primarily interested in understanding human behavior, whether deviant or normative behavior. Deterrence theory, however, is not so interested in understanding *why* people act the way they do, but rather in creating a social environment where people are compelled to obey the laws of the land.

Modern deterrence theory is most often associated with Jack Gibbs (1975). Gibbs claimed that the relative effectiveness of laws and law enforcement depends on the severity and certainty of the punishment. If a person feels that there is a high probability of being caught and punished for committing a crime (high certainty), and that the punishment will be fairly severe, that person will be deterred. This, of course, makes good theoretical sense, and a variety of empirical studies have supported this claim (Gray and Martin [1969]; Bailey, Martin, and Gray [1974]). Gibbs's theory is also consistent with arguments presented by control theorists, who similarly claim that people weigh the costs and benefits of their actions and will refrain from committing a deviant act if the likely consequences appear to outweigh the likely rewards.

Although the above list of sociological and criminological theories is far from complete, it does provide a basic overview of the main theoretical schools and aids understanding why crime rates tend to be low in modern Japanese society. It is also worth noting that, although researchers often present their own theories as being superior to other theories, and sufficient to explain a given phenomenon, there is little in these four theories that is contradictory, and much that is complementary. Indeed, it is clear that all four are useful and contribute to our understanding of criminal and deviant behavior. For example, the relationship between control theory and deterrence was briefly alluded to. Deterrence is effective to the degree that a person fears the consequences of his or her behavior, and as noted by control theorists, people with strong attachments and investments have more to lose and, therefore, are more likely to fear the consequences.

Similar relationships can be drawn between all of the above theories. Structural theories suggest that people who live in socially disorganized neighborhoods are more likely to commit crimes. This is consistent with learning theories since people who live in these neighborhoods tend to spend less time with their parents and more time with peers, many of whom are involved in nonconventional behavior. Therefore, they are more likely to learn such behavior. Also, in economically depressed areas where unemployment rates are high, people have lower investments in conventional society, and therefore less to lose if caught committing a crime. Indeed, in some depressed areas where jobs are scarce, public schools are inadequate, and crime is rampant, people are not only more likely to learn criminal behavior and supporting rationalizations, but are unlikely to be deterred by the criminal justice system since prison life might not be any worse than street life.

The main point is that these theories fit together nicely to provide us with a broad understanding of the factors that influence crime rates. Moreover, a unifying theme that runs through all of the theories is the importance of dependence, visibility, and monitoring and sanctioning. We will now consider aspects of the Japanese social structure that are relevant to this discussion.

The Japanese Social Structure
and Its Relationship to Crime

The simplest way to organize this discussion is to consider how the Japanese social structure influences crime rates from the perspective of each of the criminological theories listed above, paying special attention to issues of dependency and visibility. Although each theory, in and of itself, is insufficient for understanding why Japan has such a low crime rate, taken as a whole they provide a reasonably complete and convincing explanation.

Structural Theories

Structural theories, especially those rooted in the Chicago school (for example, Shaw and McKay [1942]; Park, Burgess, and McKenzie [1925]), tend to view urbanization as synonymous with increases in social disorganization and anomie. That is, urban areas tend to be characterized as places where normal patterns of social support and social control break down. This breakdown is often conceptualized as an attenuation of interpersonal attachments and a weakening of explicit norms governing appropriate behavior, and has been linked to a wide range of deviant behavior, particularly crime. As discussed above, the theoretical explanation provided is that people tend to be more transient in large cities: that is, they are less likely to live with or near their families, reside in stable neighborhoods, belong to local churches or other types of community-based organizations, and so forth. In general, then, there is less social integration and more anonymity so people have more personal freedom and fewer behavioral constraints in large cities.

However, several characteristics of urban Japan have served to attenuate social disorganization and anomie. First, Japan urbanized rapidly in the late nineteenth and early twentieth centuries. Therefore, what exists now in Japan are very mature urban areas with stable neighborhoods and community organizations. Second, Japan has put in place a variety of social mechanisms that both provide social support and also discourage many forms of deviance in urban areas (Bayley [1991]; Fishman and Dinitz [1989]). This latter characteristic is directly related to issues already discussed in this book. Many companies in urban areas provide familylike environments for their employees, including collective housing, health care, recreational facilities, and so on. Thus, the urban Japanese worker is likely to experience less of a sense of social isolation than urban workers in other countries. Such an extensive work-based social support system mitigates many of the problems associated with living in a large urban area. Not only does it provide for the physical and emotional needs of the employees, but as discussed in Chapter 4, it does this in such a way as to increase workers' dependence and visibility.

In addition, there are a variety of other characteristics of urban areas that serve to reduce levels of social disorganization. First, as already mentioned, the neighborhoods tend to be fairly stable. People do not move in and out of neighborhoods with great frequency. Also, Japan has a relatively even income distribution (as measured by the Gini coefficient) so that the majority of people enjoy a middle-class lifestyle (Murakami [1978]). This means Japan has few areas that are character-ized by widespread poverty. Also, a sense of community is enhanced by a variety of community-based organizations and neighborhood associa-tions *(chonaikai)* which are ubiquitous throughout Japan.

An excellent example of how large urban areas in Japan are able to pro-duce a sense of community is provided by the recent introduction of a festival in the city of Sapporo. Sapporo is a large city on the northern is-land of Hokkaido and has a population of nearly 2 million people. Like all cities in Japan, there are seasonal festivals that a large percentage of the population takes part in, but recently a new festival was introduced. Gaku Hasegawa was a student at Hokkaido University when he vaca-tioned one summer in Kochi prefecture on the island of Shikoku. That prefecture celebrates a unique dance festival called *Yosakoi-Soran.* When Hasegawa returned to Sapporo, he told his friends about the festival and began encouraging others to help him stage a similar festival in Sapporo. The concept is that people form a dance team, and they must perform an original dance wearing original costumes. Thus, the festival requires the participants to commit a great deal of time and energy in terms of prepa-ration. They must compose the dance, find appropriate music, and make the costumes. Then, of course, all members must rehearse. The first festi-val was staged in 1992, and Hasegawa managed to convince about 1,000 people to participate, forming a total of 10 dance teams (the size of the teams varied from 10 to 200 people). By 1997, after only five years, the festival boasted 183 teams and a total of 19,000 dancers. The teams usu-ally form around preexisting social groups, such as clubs, sports teams, businesses, classmates, and so on, and people now spend many months preparing their teams. During the weekend of the festival, costumed dancers can be seen throughout the city. Thus, in a very short period of time, a new "tradition" has been established. The rapid growth of the fes-tival was made possible because of the extensive network of preexisting, small social groups. By pulling these groups together into a cohesive city-wide festival, a sense of shared community has been achieved.

Finally, recall that structural theories also note the relationship be-tween unemployment rates and crime rates. Japan has, in the past forty years, had consistently low unemployment rates, among the lowest in the world. Table 6.2 displays unemployment rates in Japan, the United States, and the United Kingdom for the past forty years. As can be seen, Japan has enjoyed very high levels of employment until quite recently, and even then, the unemployment rate is low by international standards. Both the United States and United Kingdom, on the other hand, began with very low unemployment rates, which then rose steadily until peak-ing in the mid-1980s before declining more recently. The general pattern

TABLE 6.2   Unemployment Rates for the United States, United Kingdom, and Japan, 1960–1998

Year	United States	U.K.	Japan
1960	5.5	2.2	1.7
1965	4.5	2.1	1.2
1970	4.9	3.1	1.2
1975	8.5	4.6	1.9
1980	7.1	7.0	2.0
1985	7.2	11.2	2.6
1990	5.6	6.9	2.1
1995	5.6	8.7	3.2
1998	4.6	6.3	4.4

SOURCE: Bureau of Labor Statistics (1998).

has some relationship to overall crime rate patterns. In the United States, crime peaked in the 1980s and has been declining in recent years.

It has been noted by several economists that the low unemployment rates in Japan are at least partly the result of discriminatory hiring practices and statistical manipulations (Bronfenbrenner and Yasuba [1987]). Many people who are effectively shut out of the labor market, particularly women and older men, tend to drop out of the labor force rather than join the ranks of the unemployed. Thus, actual unemployment is higher than official statistics suggest. Regardless of what the "real" unemployment rates are in Japan, unemployment among young males is low. Without condoning discriminatory hiring practices that favor these young men, this type of labor market bias likely contributes to the low crime rate in Japan. By discriminating against females and older males, Japan forces a group of people out of the labor market who are unlikely to turn to crime as a result. The link between unemployment and crime is primarily a link between unemployed young males and crime (Groves and Frank [1987]).

Nevertheless, unemployment is only one factor influencing crime, and more appropriate for understanding gradual changes in crime rates within societies than for understanding broader cross-national differences. To understand cross-societal differences, one needs to consider a variety of other theories as well.

Learning Theories

We will discuss learning theories and subculture theories in greater depth in the next chapter, when we consider white-collar crimes. For our current discussion, suffice it to say that if most behavior is learned in small, intimate groups, Japanese are constrained to learn primarily normative behavior. Since so much of their time is spent in conventional groups, such as family, school, and work groups, learning and conforming to group norms typically means learning and conforming to conventional social norms. Additionally, as discussed above, operant conditioning provides an effective means of controlling and shaping behavior. Clearly, in a country like Japan, where there is high group dependence and high visibility, operant conditioning (which involves various forms of monitoring and sanctioning) is highly effective. It is also worth noting that basic socialization practices are more uniformly performed in Japan than in many other countries, particularly the United States, since, as we discussed in the previous chapter, intact, traditional families as well as multigenerational families are still fairly common in Japan. Therefore, children spend a great deal of time under the direct supervision of either their parents or grandparents.

Of course, not all groups teach socially appropriate behavior. Subculture theory deals with those closed social environments where nonconventional behavior is learned as the group norm. These subcultures exist in all countries, including Japan, where a variety of religious and criminal subcultures flourish. In such situations, the closed social environments characterized by strong dependence and normative obligations serve to promote a wide range of deviant rather than conventional behavior. This topic, however, will be discussed in the following chapter.

Control Theories

Control theories are most directly relevant to the topics discussed in this book. In fact, in the preface to the Japanese edition of his classic book, Hirschi (1995) extensively discusses Hechter and Kanazawa's solidaristic theory of social order, the theory that this book employs. He refers to this theoretical perspective as containing the same key theoretical components as control theory. Recall that control theorists believe that most people refrain from committing deviant acts for fear of the consequences. Of particular importance are interpersonal relationships and investments in conventional society. To the extent that these ties to conventional society are strong and could be damaged by committing some deviant act, people will conclude that potential costs outweigh benefits and will refrain from participating in these acts. As discussed throughout this book, the consequences of nonconventional behavior in Japan can be extreme. A person with a criminal record will be unlikely to find a spouse or a job. Indeed, one need not even look at such an extreme example to see the consequences of nonconforming behavior. A person who merely fails to display sufficient group loyalty or fulfill normative expectations is unlikely to achieve any degree of social success. Conversely, a person who is a good group member can expect to be rewarded for his or her behavior. A person who does well on college entrance exams *will* enter a good college, a person graduating from a good college *will* receive a good job, and a person who is a responsible and hardworking employee *will* receive promotions and raises. Thus, investing in conventional society makes great sense in Japan, while participating in deviant acts does not.

This might all seem commonsensical and true of all societies. But compare the social situation in Japan with that of the United States. American society is replete with options, as well as second chances, for success. A person who divorces can remarry relatively easily; a person who is fired from one job can find another; a person who is unhappy at one school can transfer to another; a person who decides at age thirty or even forty to return to school can do so; and a high school dropout with good entrepreneurial skills can become rich and successful. Even a person convicted of a crime can reenter society at some point. The relative freedom to pursue one's own goals one's own way and to recover from past mistakes is usually seen as a positive social characteristic by Americans. But it comes at a cost. The cost is that the consequence of committing a criminal or deviant act in the United States is significantly less than it is in Japan.

Furthermore, unlike Japan, the benefits of conformity are not as certain or ubiquitous. One cannot be assured that graduating from a good college will lead to a good job, or more generally, that displaying group loyalty to any group will be rewarded in time. Indeed, conforming too precisely to social or group norms carries a negative social connotation in American society. Thus, although ties to conventional society do discourage nonconventional behavior in the United States as they do in Japan, Americans tend to have weaker ties since interpersonal relationships and employment tend to be more fluid. Once again, it is evident that increased options lead to greater personal freedom, but undermine mechanisms of social control.

Finally, recall that control theorists also consider "involvement" in conventional activities to be a key to low rates of criminal and deviant behavior. That is, the less free time a person has, the less likely he or she is to become involved in nonconventional activities. As mentioned in previous chapters, Japanese students and workers have little free time. With schools and companies demanding a great time commitment that often extends well into the evening, people have little time to participate in nonconventional activities.

Theories of Deterrence

Similar to control theories, theories of deterrence focus on the cost of committing a criminal or deviant act. Rather than studying human behavior, per se, these theorists study the relative effectiveness of the criminal justice system. They are not interested in studying deviant behavior that does not break any laws, and even less interested in studying conforming behavior. They are only interested in understanding how best to ensure that laws are not broken. As mentioned above, basic research suggests that deterrence works to the extent that there is a high perceived chance of being caught committing a crime, and further, that the punishment will be severe. We will look briefly at the Japanese criminal justice system, focusing primarily on these two issues.

Japan boasts not only the lowest crime rate of any modern industrialized country, but also the highest arrest rate (i.e., clearance rate). Table 6.3 presents a cross-national comparison of arrest rates for homicide and assault. It is clear that Japan enjoys a very high success rate in locating and arresting criminal suspects.

Furthermore, once an arrest is made, conviction is likely. In most cases when the crime is not serious and it is a first offense, the perpetrator is treated lightly with a small fine if he or she confesses and expresses remorse (Haley [1986]). However, if the person does not confess, or if the crime is relatively serious, the criminal justice system can be very harsh. It is difficult to say with certainty how an individual will be treated since there is a great deal of discretionary power allotted to the police and the public prosecutor. Police will often turn their heads at certain crimes or merely issue a warning. Prosecutors, similarly, have a great deal of leeway in deciding who will and who will not be prosecuted. If the police decide to arrest a person, and the prosecutor decides to prosecute, a guilty verdict is almost assured. Actual court cases are more of a formality than a serious attempt to adjudge a person's guilt or innocence. Judges (there is effectively no jury system—all cases are decided by judges) essentially convict all people brought before them. Van Wolferen (1989) reports that 99.8 percent of all criminal cases ever prosecuted in Japan have ended in conviction.

The high arrest rate in Japan is probably owing to factors other than good police work (Smith [1985]; Tasker [1989]). Japanese police have the "luxury" of a very supportive community that often reports suspicious behavior or even turns in people who have committed crimes. This exchange of information is greatly enhanced by a network of more than 15,000 police boxes *(koban)*, which are small neighborhood police stations (Reingold [1995]). Most of these are manned twenty-four hours a day and the police are accepted as members of the local community and perform

TABLE 6.3   Percent of Reported Homicides and Assaults Cleared by Arrest

Country	Homicide	Assault
Japan	96.5	87.2
Spain	89.3	61.7
Canada	86.8	79.9
Netherlands	78.0	65.0
France	77.2	72.7
Poland	69.5	89.9
United States	67.2	57.3
Sweden	67.0	53.0

SOURCE: Interpol (1992) and Japanese National Police Agency (1993).

a variety of community services besides strict police work. Another obvious advantage to the extensive network of *koban* is the increase in police visibility and an increased ability to monitor citizen's behavior (although this is more perception than reality since police at a *koban* more often read or watch television than patrol the streets).

A more important factor contributing to the high arrest rate, which is often overlooked because it is so obvious, is the low crime rate itself. Japan has the added "luxury" of a very low crime rate, which allows police to concentrate on solving crimes that do occur. It is often the case in countries such as the United States that police must perform a type of triage, having to rank crimes by their seriousness and then decide which to investigate and which to ignore. There are simply too many crimes and too few police.

These statistics are important since, as stated earlier, deterrence is only effective when there is a high certainty of being caught. This is, after all, commonsensical. It is difficult to scare people into compliance with the law if they do not believe they will actually be caught and punished. Thus, the higher the arrest rate, the higher the certainty of being caught committing a crime. The above statistics suggest that in general there is a higher certainty that a Japanese person committing a crime will be caught than there is for a citizen of most other countries.

Indeed, the likelihood that an American committing a crime will be caught is extremely low. Using estimates from victimization surveys, the U.S. Bureau of Justice reports that only a small fraction of crimes are ever reported to the police in the first place. Even if we concentrate on the most serious category of crimes, felonies, only about half are ever reported to the police. Therefore, a person committing a felony has a fifty-fifty chance that the crime will not even be reported. Furthermore, of those reported, less than half will result in arrest and only a small percentage of those arrested will end in conviction. Thus, potential criminals can correctly believe that it is quite unlikely they will pay a heavy price for their actions.

The situation described here suggests an interesting type of social dynamic. As long as the crime rate is low, police are able to arrest a high percentage of those people committing crimes. This, in turn, leads to a high certainty of being caught, which makes efforts at deterrence more effective, thus keeping the crime rate low. However, if the crime rate begins to rise (due to increased unemployment rates, a weakening of informal social control mechanisms, or so on), the police are less able to apprehend the majority of perpetrators, which then lowers the certainty of being caught, undermining the ability of a society to deter potential criminals. Or put more simply, it is much easier to maintain a low crime rate than it is to bring down a high crime rate (something the United States and many other countries would readily attest to).

Finally, recall that the second factor related to the effectiveness of deterrence is severity of punishment. It would be misleading to think of this factor only in terms of sentencing practices; in that case, Japan would appear to be a very lenient country. Table 6.4 compares a variety of countries in terms of the percent of people convicted of crimes who are sentenced to prison and the average length of a prison sentence. These statistics suggest that Japan, along with the United Kingdom, Finland, and perhaps Canada, are quite lenient, whereas Mexico, the United States, the Netherlands, and the Russian Federation tend to be severe.

Although there is some truth to these findings (certainly one would be well advised *not* to commit a crime in Mexico), these statistics do not tell the whole story.

First, it should be remembered that "certainty" plays a crucial role in deterrence. Despite severe sentences, if there is a low perceived chance of being caught in the first place, potential criminals are unlikely to be deterred. Second, the actual cost of being caught committing a crime extends beyond the sentence meted out. And the cost in Japan is very high. Regardless of the length of prison time, a person with a criminal record will find it almost impossible to reenter Japanese society. One's group affiliations will have been severed, and establishing new affiliations, whether in terms of an occupation or even interpersonal relationships, is extremely difficult. The cost can also be measured in psychological or emotional terms, in the form of shame and disgrace. Being caught committing a crime not only disgraces the individual, but also reflects poorly on the person's friends, family, and professional colleagues. Thus, one not only feels personal embarrassment, but also must deal with having brought shame and embarrassment to others. Indeed, it is this aspect of Japanese society that some researchers claim is largely responsible for the low crime rate (Braithwaite [1989]; Bayley [1991]).

TABLE 6.4   Severity of Sentencing Practices

Country	Percent Sentenced to Prison	Average Length of Sentence (in weeks)
Japan	2	90
U.K.	4	25
Finland	10	37
Switzerland	18	107
Belgium	26	82
Canada	30	4
Russian Federation	37	260
Netherlands	45	149
United States	60	117
Mexico	92	831

SOURCE: United Nations World Crime Survey (1995).

Conclusion

Obviously, the study of crime is complex and many factors contribute to a society's overall crime rate. In this chapter, we reviewed what most criminologists would claim are the main factors, and related them to how they fit in with elements of the Japanese social structure that were discussed in previous chapters.

First, we reviewed structural theories and noted that Japan's low level of unemployment for young males contributes to its low crime rate. In Chapters 4 and 5 we noted some of the ways Japan maintains those low unemployment rates. Here we see how criminological theories predict its relevance to social order. Also, we noted how structural theorists claim that crime is related to a breakdown in social support systems and the increased anonymity that comes with urbanization. But, as we discussed in Chapters 3 and 4, the extensive network of closed, tight-knit small groups throughout Japanese society ensure that people have adequate social support networks and are constantly kept in high visibility environments. Thus, life in Japan, even in urban Japan, more closely mirrors rural life in other countries than it does urban life, and is subject to the benefits of rural life (e.g., safety and security) and also its drawbacks (e.g., a lack of personal freedom and opportunities).

Second, we discussed learning theories, which claim crime and deviant behavior are learned in primary groups. Again, Chapters 3, 4, and 5 show how socialization within Japanese groups is taught and maintained. High dependence and a lack of alternative means for success ensure that most people will learn and exhibit normative behavior. Further, learning theories stress the importance of an effective reward and punishment system (operant conditioning). Throughout this book we have demonstrated how effective Japanese groups are at monitoring and sanctioning inappropriate behavior.

Third, we discussed control theories, which predicts that people who have strong ties to conventional society will refrain from participating in criminal or deviant acts because of a fear of injuring those ties. Again, the relevance of this criminological theory to the topics discussed in previous chapters is clear. Most Japanese have strong ties to conventional society, and the damage done to those ties by acting inappropriately can be irreparable. Moreover, control theorists also note the importance of time, claiming that people who are busy in conventional activities simply do not have time to participate in nonconventional activities. This is a point we have made repeatedly throughout this book. Japanese people, especially youths, are kept very busy.

Finally, we discussed deterrence theory, and the role of the criminal justice system in deterring potential criminals. The effectiveness of this system is also related to issues discussed in this book. Since deterrence is most effective when the cost of being caught committing a crime is high, the fact that the social structure is so unforgiving allows the criminal justice system to effectively deter potential criminals. Reestablishing any type of normal life after being caught and convicted of a crime is a daunting task, daunting enough to instill in most people a strong desire to avoid that possibility.

The above discussion highlights the role small-group dependency and visibility plays in keeping crime rates low. Since many people are highly dependent on conventional groups and must conform to the group's normative requirements, virtually all forms of deviant behavior, including criminal behavior, are curbed. The high visibility setting that most people live in ensures that clandestine deviant behavior is kept to a minimum. Further, since being a good group member usually leads to future rewards, ties to conventional society are strong, making the cost of committing an illegal act high. Therefore, it is no wonder that the Japanese crime rate remains low. However, it is important to remember that we have, thus far, only discussed street crimes. Other crimes, such as certain types of white-collar or professional crimes, do not necessarily follow the same pattern. Indeed, the same social structure that discourages street crimes might actually encourage other types of crimes. We will now turn to that topic.

PART THREE

Nonintuitive Consequences

7

Crime Revisited:
White-Collar Crimes

The previous chapter focused exclusively on what could be termed "street crimes" and "violent crimes." However, although the social structure described in this book might attenuate these types of crime, it might actually foster other types of crime. Dependence on any group, even conventional groups, can easily lead to a situation where one is required by the group to perform some illegal or immoral act. After all, a corollary of the type of group dynamics we have described throughout this book is that the interest of the group should supercede the interest of the individual. Thus, a typical feature of tight-knit, small groups is that behavior is evaluated in terms of whether it promotes group interests, not whether it is socially normative. Obviously there is an inherent danger in such a perspective.

As was pointed out in the previous chapter's discussion of subcultures, deviant behavior can be thought of similarly to conventional behavior in terms of learning and socialization patterns, the only difference being the social context. People who are socialized into a conventional group will exhibit socially normative behavior whereas people who are socialized into a nonconventional group will exhibit socially deviant behavior. Examples of conventional groups might be school-related groups, conventional church groups, and so on. Nonconventional groups might include street gangs or religious cults. The main point is that the actual process of acquiring certain behaviors does not differ for these groups. It involves basic socialization processes such as modeling, operant conditioning, internalizing group values, and so on. The more tight-knit and closed the group is, the more likely a group member's behavior will conform to group norms, whatever those norms might be. Or put in terms of the theoretical orientation of this book, the greater a member's dependence is on the group, and the more visible he or she is to other group members, the more likely it is that he or she will conform to group norms.

Throughout this book we have assumed that the groups were all conventional groups: school, work, neighborhood, and family. However, there are, of course, nonconventional groups in Japan. Attracting a fair amount of media attention are various religious cults such as Aum Shinrikyo, the *yakuza* (organized crime syndicates), and even some youth gangs. And as one would expect, they, too, tend to be tight-knit, closed groups that demand and command normative obligations and behavioral conformity. And also as one would expect, much of the behavior nonconventional groups demand from their members is socially deviant. However, these groups are not particularly unique to Japan. Virtually all modern societies have similar types of nonconventional groups, and the social processes that operate within these groups are similar from society to society. Thus, whatever country one is in, cult behavior or gang behavior tends to be quite similar—people exhibit strong loyalty to their group and maintain a strong sense of identity, commitment, and behavioral conformity. Japan is not unique in this regard. What is unique in Japan is that the same pattern also applies to conventional groups.

Furthermore, although conventional groups might inhibit certain types of illegal behavior, they might encourage other types of illegal behavior, especially if the behavior is aimed at furthering group goals. Remember that the goal of small groups is neither social order nor the promotion of social norms. Rather, social order is an unintended consequence since group conformity often inhibits various forms of socially inappropriate behavior (specifically, common street crimes and violent criminal behavior). However, it is not unusual for group goals to foster other types of socially inappropriate behavior. Given the closed social environment many groups operate in, the degree of group cohesiveness and loyalty they maintain, and the severe consequences of doing or saying anything that might put one at odds with other group members, there is little in the way of "external checks." Although monitoring and sanctioning is a common feature of small groups, it is always *internal* monitoring and sanctioning. Group members' behavior is usually not subject to the scrutiny of people outside of the group. This "secretive" element of many small groups, combined with the competitive nature and pressure to show profits that characterize many modern businesses, likely creates an environment where certain subcultural norms can develop, norms where certain types of illegal behavior become "standard operating procedure."

Refining Our Concept of White-Collar Crime

The term "white-collar crime," originally coined by Edwin Sutherland in 1939, quite literally referred to crimes committed by people of higher social status in the course of their occupation. However, its popular usage has expanded to include virtually all types of crimes other than common street crimes. This includes a broad array of illegal acts from bribery and fraud to environmental pollution and unsafe working conditions. These acts are so broad that they include crimes not directly related to a person's work, such as cheating on one's income taxes, to crimes not limited to middle- or upper-class people, such as writing bad checks. Some distinctions and refinements are necessary to highlight white-collar crimes that are relevant to our current discussion.

Past research in the field of white-collar crime has sometimes distinguished between white-collar crimes committed by an individual for personal gain and those committed with the intention of advancing the goals of the organization (see Coleman [1985]; Hamilton and Sanders [1996]; Clinard and Quinney [1973]). Such a distinction is particularly appropriate to the current discussion of white-collar crimes. One would expect the former to be lower in Japan than in other countries since high visibility prevents people from conducting clandestine acts aimed at personal gain. However, the latter would be expected to be higher in Japan than elsewhere since group solidarity and loyalty are ubiquitous characteristics of Japanese social life.

Unfortunately, empirical support for this proposition is hard to come by. White-collar crimes, almost by definition, are hidden. Most white-collar crime goes unreported to the police since there is often no clear victim (at least in the sense that there is a victim in the case of a robbery or assault). Rather, victims of white-collar crimes tend to be large organizations (such as insurance companies, government agencies, and so on) or the public in general (Goode [1990]). Or put in criminological terms, white-collar crimes require *proactive* rather than *reactive* law enforcement (Hagan [1994]). The police must try to actively uncover a crime rather than merely respond to the report of one. This makes it extremely difficult to quantify white-collar crimes, especially from a cross-national perspective. All of the caveats discussed in the previous chapter concerning common street crimes are multiplied. Differences in the degree to which white-collar criminals are pursued, arrested, and convicted vary greatly from country to country. Also, laws concerning a great many related issues, such as environmental protection, consumer fraud, occupational safety laws, collusion, and so on also differ from country to country, so what is illegal in one country might not be illegal in another.

Despite these many limitations, the topic is of great importance and worth considering, even with the empirical limitations. Two white-collar crimes that are routinely reported in international crime statistics are fraud and embezzlement. These two crimes typically fall into the category of crimes committed for personal gain; therefore, we would expect Japan to exhibit relatively low rates. Table 7.1 presents rates for these two

TABLE 7.1   Cross-National Comparison of Fraud and Embezzlement Rates

Country	Fraud	Embezzlement
Sweden	568.76	104.89
Scotland	426.60	6.92
Austria	401.61	40.09
Canada	352.88	—
Finland	306.05	72.54
Korea	282.70	45.59
Hungary	256.27	44.70
England	253.82	—
Denmark	195.60	20.06
France	174.53	—
Japan	41.71	1.50

SOURCE: United Nations World Crime Survey (1995).

crimes for a variety of countries (note that the United States did not provide information on these crimes for the United Nations survey). As expected, Japan appears to have relatively low rates of fraud and embezzlement.

Identifying the degree to which crimes committed to benefit a company occur is much more difficult. Indeed, it is even difficult to accurately distinguish those crimes committed to benefit the individual and
those committed to benefit the company. For owners, upper management, and stockholders, oftentimes what benefits the company benefits
the individual as well. Even for lower-level employees, aiding the company through illegal acts, or loyally standing by others who commit illegal acts might be individually rewarded in the long run in the form of
raises or promotions. Thus, the distinction made above is not nearly as
clear as it appears. Nevertheless, it is a useful way to think about how
certain forms of social structures interact with certain types of criminal
behavior.

It is interesting here to note that despite Japan's well-earned reputation
as an extremely safe and orderly society, that positive reputation does not
extend to cover images of corruption. A series of international surveys
aimed at ascertaining images of corruption were conducted in 1998 by a
group known as Transparency International. They created a "corruption
perception index" based on data from up to twelve separate surveys of
people from around the world who were involved in international business. The index rates each country in terms of how "clean" or "corrupt"
the international business community perceives the country. Results of
this research for a variety of modern industrialized countries are pres-

TABLE 7.2   International Comparison of Perceived Corruption

Country	Score[a]
Denmark	10.0
Sweden	9.5
Canada	9.2
Netherlands	9.0
Norway	9.0
Australia	8.7
U.K.	8.7
Germany	7.9
Hong Kong	7.8
Austria	7.5
United States	7.5
France	6.7
Spain	6.1
Japan	5.8
Italy	4.6
South Korea	4.2

[a]The range is from 0 (highly corrupt) to 10 (highly clean).
SOURCE: Transparency International (1998).

ented in Table 7.2. As can be seen, Denmark ranks highest, followed by Sweden and Canada. Japan, however, does not fare well, with only Italy and South Korea being perceived as more corrupt.

These results illustrate graphically the need to distinguish between street crime and white-collar crime. No doubt people involved in international business know how safe and orderly Japanese society is. Yet this knowledge has no particular relevance when assessing issues of corruption. Indeed, the relationship between crime rates in general and perceptions of corruption appear to be unrelated. Furthermore, these results highlight the importance of distinguishing between different types of white-collar crimes. Crimes committed for personal gain appear to have no relation to the more structural charge of corruption. This is most clearly evident in the case of Sweden, which has the highest levels of fraud and embezzlement, but is still perceived as one of the "cleanest" societies in which to do business.

Companies as Subcultures

It is not unusual among white-collar crime researchers to treat companies as deviant subcultures. A typical description of a subculture is a group of people who have close contact with one another, see themselves as belonging to a unique group, often characterized by a special way of dressing, and who learn a set of norms and values that differentiate themselves from other groups. It is easy to see how this description can fit some companies as well as it does gangs or religious groups. It is often the case that work groups define very clearly what is acceptable and what is unacceptable behavior, and new employees are quickly socialized into this environment and conform to behavioral expectations. Further, it seems self-evident that the more close-knit and interdependent the employees are, the stronger the pressure to conform to group behavioral norms. A good example is provided by McCaghy and Capron (1997) in their discussion concerning the prevalence of police corruption. They offer the following explanation:

> This indifference of police toward corruption in their own ranks is not simply the result of misplaced loyalty. Rather, it indicates the solidarity of police that emerges as a necessary element of the job. . . . Police work in tight, informal groups and see themselves as operating alone against an uninformed and indifferent, if not hostile, world. Any illegal practices that emerge within police groups can develop into secret standards for the groups. These standards are perpetuated by being passed on to recruits coming into the ranks. Should a recruit resist participation, group acceptance will be withheld, and the recruit will experience isolation because of his or her lack of group "loyalty." (245–246)

Similar examples abound. In a fascinating study of national securities markets, Baker (1984) notes how traders in the pits organize themselves into tight-knit social groups that favor members of the same pit, refusing to hear or accept better bids made from traders from other pits. These examples show how tight-knit groups develop a type of subculture, where group goals are placed above rules of proper behavior. It is not hard to see how a similar dynamic might operate in a great many group settings across Japan. Consider the results presented in Tables 7.3 and 7.4 from the 1991 World Values Survey. Table 7.3 present the percent of respondents who answered that "they would have to be convinced" before obeying questionable orders from superiors at work. Although in many countries nearly half the respondents replied that they would not follow their superiors' orders unless they were convinced that doing so was right, only about 11 percent of the Japanese respondents responded similarly. Obviously, many Japanese feel they are not in a position to question their superiors at work. Interestingly, the United States was second lowest, with only about 23 percent answering this way.

TABLE 7.3   Percent Who Must Be Convinced Before Following
Questionable Orders

Country	Percent
Denmark	53.7
Spain	50.4
Korea	47.8
France	47.5
Netherlands	47.3
Italy	46.9
Belgium	45.0
U.K.	43.1
Sweden	41.4
Canada	28.6
West Germany	23.8
United States	23.1
Japan	10.9

SOURCE: World Values Survey (1991).

TABLE 7.4   How Much Control Do You Have Over Your Own Life (0–10)?

Country	Mean
United States	7.57
Canada	7.55
Korea	7.53
Sweden	7.48
Denmark	7.02
U.K.	7.00
West Germany	6.96
Spain	6.76
Belgium	6.55
Italy	6.52
France	6.24
Netherlands	6.18
Japan	5.47

SOURCE: World Values Survey (1991).

Table 7.4 presents results of a question that asks respondents how
much control they feel they have over their lives. The responses were on
a scale from one to ten, ten indicating a great deal of personal control.
Once again, Japan represents the extreme end of the continuum, with respondents claiming to have less control over their own lives than do re-

spondents from all other countries. This time the United States and Japan represent polar opposites.

Given this situation, it is easy to see how abuses are possible in Japan. Individuals often have no choice but to make a long-term commitment to a very tight-knit group where they are dependent on group leaders and have little autonomy. Thus, John Braithwaite (1989) notes that Japan provides an excellent example of not only a society with low street crime, but also a society with "white collar criminal subcultures of unusual coherence" (136). He goes on to note that "None of this should surprise us. After all, Japanese communitarianism is also manifested in common criminal gangs that are more highly organized, more capable of exacting total loyalty from their members, to follow directions to engage in crime, than criminal gangs found in most of the rest of the world" (137). Other researchers familiar with crime patterns in Japan also claim that white-collar crime is rampant, despite the lack of empirical evidence (see, for example, van Wolferen [1989]; Woronoff [1980]).

Examples of White-Collar Crime in Japan

As mentioned above, it is very hard to put one's finger on white-collar crimes or to quantify their occurrences. However, it is not much of an exaggeration to state that one can hardly open a newspaper in Japan without reading about the latest political or business-related scandal. Of course, there is no way to know whether Japan is unique in this regard. These types of crimes might be exceedingly common in many countries, but do not come to light as frequently as they do in Japan. However, even if Japan is not exceptional in this regard, this fact alone, given the exceptionally low rates of all other measurable forms of deviant behavior, is noteworthy. Whatever social structural processes serve to attenuate other forms of criminal and deviant behavior do not appear to significantly impact certain types of white-collar crimes.

Before discussing specific examples, though, it is necessary to add one important element to the discussion of the characteristics of white-collar crime. Although this chapter's focus is on crimes that benefit the group and on normative obligations that encourage such behavior, it is often the case that such actions necessarily involve collusion with other groups. Of course, one can act in a strictly predatory fashion, but often a better strategy is to forge alliances with important business and political leaders. Thus, one sees the prevalence of such white-collar crimes as insider trading, bribery, and price fixing. In this regard, the importance of the *keiretsu* is clear. The *keiretsu* is a fairly tight-knit group composed of the top executives from various corporations. Thus, yet another group is made up of leaders of smaller groups. The advantages of this type of "cooperative" arrangement are obvious, as are the temptations to misuse it. Consider, for example, that it has been estimated that 70 percent of all corporate stock in Japan is owned by other corporations rather than by individuals (Dore [1987]).

A brief summary of some of the major news stories of the 1990s will serve to illustrate this point. On the political front, the early 1990s were highlighted by several major scandals involving the then-ruling Liberal Democratic Party (LDP). Reports began circulating that many of the companies that became successful after World War II did so through clandestine relations with the LDP. Among them was Sagawa Kyubin, Japan's largest parcel delivery service. Sagawa Kyubin had evidently bribed several key LDP politicians to gain favorable policies aiding its establishment. Similar allegations concerning illegal political contributions to the LDP have been raised regularly. In 1992, investigators uncovered a host of illegal activities by Shin Kanemaru, the behind-the-scenes leader of the LDP. He was not only implicated in illegal activities involving influence peddling, but was also tied to organized crime. This particular scandal contributed to the LDP losing power in 1993 and Morihiro Hosokawa assuming the role of prime minister. Unfortunately, his tenure lasted only until 1994, when he was forced to resign from office because of his own scandal involving a series of dubious loans he was involved with in the 1980s.

One of the few studies to address white-collar crime in Japan was conducted by Kerbo and Inoue (1990). Similar to our observations, the authors find the route of such corruption in the social structure, specifically strong group ties and loyalty combined with fierce competition. They claim "the importance of small group organization and its characteristics may at times provide social support for the rationalization of white collar crime in Japan, as well as carrying it out in a way that is more difficult to detect" (142). They focus on the *keiretsu* and claim that although competition thrives in Japan, success is still best achieved through carefully fostering social relationships and entering into a network of long-term reciprocal exchanges. Although these networks tend to involve elite from a variety of organizations, the elite themselves are not capable of single-handedly carrying out elaborate exchanges. They typically need the backing of their respective organizations and the cooperation of their subordinates. It is in this sense that the nature of organizations, especially the high dependence of workers leading to high normative obligations, plays an important role in making such transactions viable.

On the more recent business front, Japan has fared no better. Many of the economic problems Japan has experienced in the 1990s are related to the banking industry, which has made a series of questionable investments and bad loans and then tried to cover up its losses. By early 1998 the Finance Ministry reported that Japanese banks had incurred $610 billion of debt. Furthermore, the Finance Ministry itself became embroiled in a scandal that eventually led to the resignation of several senior bureaucrats as well as the arrest of several employees. Evidently, bank inspectors were being bribed, and in return they were tipping off the banks as to when the ministry would conduct surprise inspections, thus giving banks time to conceal information concerning bad loans. Even the Bank of Japan was eventually implicated in the scandal.

None of these are isolated incidents. Nor do they exhaust even the major scandals of the decade, let alone smaller scandals. There have also been recent charges of insider trading, unfair government procurement practices, and influence peddling against such major agencies as the Ministry of Health and Welfare and the Japanese Defense Ministry. It should also be noted that there is nothing exceptional about the 1990s. Scandals involving clandestine relationships among Japan's large power brokers have been a mainstay of contemporary Japanese society. What they have in common is that they typically involve long-term reciprocal exchanges among people in power. Such acts seem more commonplace in Japan than the more individualistic white-collar crimes such as embezzlement and fraud.

Moreover, if the crime is committed primarily to benefit the organization rather than an individual, it is often treated differently by the criminal justice system. A typical example involves the rash of banking scandals that have occurred in the mid- to late 1990s. Faced with a large number of bad loans, many banking executives chose to conceal their banks' debts, thus protecting both the investors and the banks' reputation. A particularly blatant illegal attempt to do this involved Hokkoku Bank in Kanazawa. The president of the bank attempted to defraud the prefecture's credit insurance association of 80 million yen to cover the bank's debts. Although the president of the bank was found guilty, the judge suspended the sentence on the grounds that he did not commit the crime for personal benefit but for the benefit of the bank.

Examples of white-collar crimes are not limited to business and politics. If closed, hierarchical social groups are characterized by clandestine activities, one would expect the sumo world to be a prime candidate for such abuses. People normally enter the sumo community at a young age and stay in it for their entire lives. Sumo wrestlers live and train together, and rarely interact with the outside world. They represent an extreme form of a closed, hierarchical group, where members are completely dependent on the group and live in a high visibility, highly regulated environment. Even after retiring from active competition, everyone is expected to stay in the organization in some capacity.

Indeed, if one opts to leave, one is banned from the sumo community for life.

As with many forms of Japanese life, the web of social relationships in sumo operates on two distinct levels. First, each wrestler is a member of a stable, and within the stable there is a strict hierarchy: lower-level members cater to the whims and demands of the higher-ranking members, who in turn are strictly obedient to the elder head of the stable. The members, besides training together, live, eat, and sleep communally. Presumably to protect against fixing bouts, members of the same stable do not fight one another during tournaments (except on rare occasions when the tournament ends in a tie involving two members of the same stable). And generally speaking, each stable is in competition with the others to produce the highest-ranking wrestlers. However, as in business, a type of *keiretsu* exists among the heads of the stables, and also as in business, it makes sense to sometimes "agree" rather than compete.

Given the closed nature of the organization, the strong interpersonal ties among all of the participants, and the lack of any form of external monitoring of bouts, one would naturally assume there to be some abuses. Indeed, sumo has long been suspected of occasionally fixing bouts. Although allegations have never been proven or admitted to by the Japan Sumo Association, rumors have persisted and the topic has even been discussed on a number of occasions by members of the Diet (Schilling [1994]). The *Shukan Post*, a weekly tabloid, routinely runs stories claiming that bouts are occasionally fixed, and although their stories are not always credible, some wrestlers have come forward and admitted that they have thrown bouts in the past. Of course, given the lack of any external controls and the intense loyalty and close relations among all of the participants, it would be surprising if there were no back room politicking going on.

Conclusion

Americans are often puzzled by the difficulty of doing business in Japan and the prevalence of what they feel are unfair business practices and disregard for international law. The puzzlement comes, in part, by the strong perceptions of Japanese as law-abiding people. In this chapter we have suggested why this paradox exists. We began by noting a likely irony concerning the relationship between the Japanese social structure and crime. The same processes that serve to discourage one type of crime might actually foster another type. Since most research in the field of criminology focuses on "street crime," Japan enjoys the reputation of being a safe and orderly country characterized by unusually low crime rates. This reputation is well earned, and visitors to Japan often marvel at the degree of safety they enjoy during their stay in the country. However, street crime is only one category of criminal activity, and it appears Japan does not fare so well in other categories. Although intense group affiliations characterized by high dependence and high visibility tend to prevent most people from going out and robbing liquor stores or taking drugs, it likely encourages certain types of white-collar crimes, particularly crimes committed in the course of one's work to benefit one's company.

Although white-collar crime is inherently difficult to study, a variety of factors suggest that, unlike street crime, Japan cannot boast of low levels of white-collar crime. Since only a fraction of actual white-collar crimes are ever uncovered and newspapers in Japan almost daily report such crimes, one can assume actual levels are quite high. Furthermore, there are good theoretical reasons to believe that these types of crime are high in Japan. As shown in the World Values Survey, Japanese respondents claim to have little personal control over their lives and feel compelled to follow the orders of their superiors. Further, given a social structure characterized by intense group loyalty among workers and long-term, reciprocal exchanges among the elite in politics and business, it would be surprising if white-collar crimes did *not* exist in Japan.

This chapter was not meant to provide an all-encompassing discussion of white-collar crime. The topic is far too broad. We chose to ignore a variety of related crimes such as environmental issues and worker safety, and also did not discuss Japanese organized crime (the *yakuza*). We also downplayed the degree to which white-collar crimes are committed for personal profit. The reason was not to downplay the importance of these issues, but rather to highlight the dual nature of social order and social control. Once again, we see that social order is a two-edged sword, and the same social control methods that lead to positive social consequences also produce unintended negative social consequences.

8

The Religious Landscape of Japan

We have already discussed some of the unintended consequences of a social structure that produces high degrees of order and conformity through small-group social control mechanisms. These consequences, although unintended, are fairly obvious: low crime and delinquency, low levels of creativity, and so on. However, the effects of this system go well beyond the obvious. Because of the high level of group dependence and its accompanying obligations, little in life is left unaffected. One lives in a relatively closed social network where behavior is carefully monitored and, if necessary, sanctioned. In return for this commitment, group members receive a great many social benefits, and it is in this regard that religion and religious behavior are affected.

To understand how primary group interactions have affected the development of both the religious landscape of Japan and individual religiosity, we will begin with a brief discussion of religion in modern Japan. The purpose of this discussion is not to give a detailed account of religious beliefs or practices, but to highlight broad characteristics of religious life in Japan. As will be seen, the key to understanding religious life in modern Japan lies in understanding primary group interactions.

Religion in Japan

Westerners often view Japan as a highly secularized society and the Japanese as a highly nonreligious people. The reason for this is largely based on two observations: first, religious behavior is confined to specific (and infrequent) life events, rather than expressive in the course of one's everyday life; second, cross-national survey research suggests that Japanese people rank among the lowest internationally on various measures of religiosity. A typical cross-national comparison can be seen in Table 8.1.

It is easy to conclude from these types of international surveys that Japan has a very low level of religiosity vis-à-vis other industrialized

TABLE 8.1   Percent Answering "Yes" to Typical Religion Questions

Country	*I Am a Religious Person*	*I Attend Religious Services at Least Once a Month*
South Korea	—	64
United States	84	59
Italy	84	51
Switzerland	73	42
Canada	71	40
Belgium	69	35
Spain	67	40
West Germany	65	33
Netherlands	61	31
Great Britain	57	24
France	51	17
Japan	26	14

SOURCE: World Values Survey (1991).

countries. However, regardless of the statistics presented in Table 8.1, it is not necessarily accurate to conclude that Japan is a nonreligious country. The reason is that the questions asked in Table 8.1 are very much religion-specific. If a religious tradition does not require certain behaviors, or even beliefs, it would be foolish to use them as a measure of religiosity within that tradition. To do so would be tantamount to claiming Jews are less religious than Catholics because they do not take communion. In actuality, Japanese religions do not require attendance at services, nor do they even require a person to express any beliefs. Furthermore, the first question asked in Table 8.1 is interpreted differently by Japanese than it is by Westerners. A "religious person" by Japanese definition is a person who is an active member of a religious organization. Table 8.1 shows approximately 26 percent of Japanese people claim to be active members of a religious group. Thus, a person might hold a variety of "religious" beliefs but still reply that he or she is "not a religious person."

Consider now the survey results presented in Table 8.2. These survey questions cover a wider range of beliefs, all of which could be termed "religious" beliefs. A different picture emerges. From these survey results, one can see that a fairly large percentage of Japanese people hold "religious" beliefs. Indeed, Japan no longer appears to be a religious outlier among the modern industrialized countries. If anything, Japan appears quite religious, with a higher percentage of Japanese believing in an afterlife than their British, French, German, Dutch, Spanish, or Belgian counterparts. Similarly, belief in a soul is fairly high in Japan, higher than

TABLE 8.2   Percent Answering "Yes" to Other Questions on Religiosity

| | Belief in | | |
Country	a God	an Afterlife	a Soul
United States	96	78	92
Italy	90	68	77
Switzerland	—	64	81
Canada	89	69	85
Belgium	71	45	61
Spain	86	51	67
West Germany	78	50	74
Netherlands	65	45	72
Denmark	64	34	47
Great Britain	79	53	71
France	62	44	55
Japan	65	54	75

SOURCE: World Values Survey (1991).

it is in France, Great Britain, Denmark, the Netherlands, Germany, Spain, or Belgium. If anything, it is more appropriate to claim that it is the United States, rather than Japan, that is the outlier, because of its unusually high level of religiosity.

There appears, then, to be a paradox. On the one hand a fairly large percentage of Japanese people express some form of religiosity, while on the other hand, religion has little influence in their day-to-day lives, and religious organizations do little to promote more active organizational involvement. To better understand this paradox, we will briefly describe when and how religion does manifest itself in the lives of most modern Japanese.

Although religious life in Japan is a syncretism of several different religious traditions, including elements of Taoism and Confucianism, the two main religious traditions are Shinto and Buddhism. Shinto, the only indigenous religion of Japan, has historically consisted of loosely-held folk beliefs, with little formal organizational structure. Indeed, it did not even have a name until the appearance of Buddhism in the seventh century (Earhart [1982]; Hori et al. [1972]). Associated with Shinto are a variety of animistic beliefs, that is, beliefs that spirits can be found throughout nature (Earhart [1984]; Clyde and Beers [1975]). Historically, there have been periodic attempts to codify Shinto's beliefs and practices, and develop more of an organizational structure. This was usually attempted during times of political turmoil to add legitimacy to the ruling elite. A good example comes from the eighth century when political authorities introduced the creation myth into Shinto teachings in order to bolster imperial rule. This myth taught that Japan was created by the sun goddess Amaterasu, who was the ancestress of the Yamato clan, the lineage from which the emperors emerged (Hori et al. [1972]). This provided the rule of the Yamato clan (and all subsequent emperors in this lineage) with a spiritual legitimacy. Of course, a more recent attempt to organize Shinto and use it as a political tool came in the early part of this century. Referred to by historians as State-Shinto, it essentially involved a similar strategy to promote loyalty to the emperor (see Smith [1985] for an excellent discussion of this).

In post–World War II Japan, however, there is little organizational structure to Shinto. It has essentially returned to its original form: a syncretism of various folk beliefs and practices. It has little or no specific religious doctrines, nor is any specific religious behavior required of Japanese people, other than normative moral expectations (Kitagawa [1987]; Ishida [1971]; Miller [1991]). Thus, there are no "members" in the sense that Westerners would use the term, nor are there regular meetings where religious issues are discussed. Instead, a collection of rituals exist to be performed by Shinto priests on specific occasions, such as during weddings, after the birth of a child, to aid individuals in times of crisis, and in association with various calendar festivals. In other words, Shinto is a service industry, providing specific religious services to those who desire it (Miller [1992a]). Further, even for those who participate in the rituals, Shinto teaches that the efficacy of a ritual is related only to the accuracy with which it is performed. Any additional theological knowledge or belief is unnecessary, even for the priests themselves (Hardacre [1984]).

Buddhism, of course, has a very different history, entering Japan with a firm organizational structure and developed theological system of beliefs. Over time, it spawned many sects and gathered a significant following throughout Japan, ultimately being named the official state religion of the Tokugawa Shogunate in the seventeenth century (Murakami [1968]; Holtom [1963]). In Tokugawa life, Buddhist teachings and beliefs dominated social life, leading to various rules of conduct and a social caste system that was strictly adhered to during the 200-year Tokugawa reign.

With the rise of State-Shinto during the Meiji Restoration period of the late nineteenth century, Buddhism lost its political backing and much of its popular support. It became relegated to performing funeral services and overseeing rituals involving the care of ancestral spirits. With the exception of a variety of "New Religions" (primarily Buddhist sectarian groups), Buddhism remains largely in the background for most Japanese, only surfacing when individuals need the specific services it provides

(Miller [1992a, 1995]; Morioka [1975a]). Thus, in modern Japanese society, Shinto and Buddhism do not typically compete with one another for adherents, as religious groups might do in most other countries, but instead provide various religious services such as overseeing rituals and ceremonies, providing prayers and good luck charms, and so on, that Japanese people avail themselves of as the need arises (Miller [1992a]; Morioka [1975b]).

What currently exists in Japan, then, is a religious landscape that looks quite different from the United States (or a variety of other Western and Eastern societies). Although U.S. religious organizations compete with one another for adherents and require acceptance of various beliefs and at least a minimum amount of personal commitment, Japanese religions operate quite differently. They are primarily nonmembership organizations that do not ask for, or require, individual acceptance or commitment. Japanese religions remain largely in the background and offer a host of spiritual services to people who request them.

The standard reasons given to explain these differences are not convincing. Some researchers have focused on theological differences, using Max Weber's classic work on religion to support their claims. Weber (1968 [1922]), in an attempt to explain differences in Western and Eastern religion, especially as they are related to understanding why capitalism arose in the West rather than the East, claimed that Western religions tended to be "this-worldly" in their orientation, whereas Eastern religions were "other-worldly." If this were true, one might conclude that it is only natural for Eastern religions to attract only a small following of strict adherents, those people willing to abandon secular life for monastic life. Unfortunately, Weber's characterization of Western and Eastern religions was not very accurate. Buddhism on the popular level, especially the forms of Buddhism that flourished in China and Japan (i.e., the Mahayana branch), has always been very "this-worldly," emphasizing the use of Buddhist chanting and rituals to obtain very concrete practical results (such as a better job, success in marriage, good grades in school, and so on). The only exception to this, of course, is its overseeing of funerals, which is decidedly other-worldly, but no more so than Western religions, which all oversee funerals as well.

It is also insufficient to claim that "Japanese religions" have some unique characteristics that do not permit them to develop into competing membership-based organizations. As mentioned above, throughout much of Japanese history religious groups were very well organized and extremely competitive (see Anesaki [1930] for an extensive history of religious organizations in Japan). Thus, it is difficult to claim that it is the "nature of Japanese religion" that is responsible for understanding the lack of importance religion currently plays in the daily lives of the Japanese. Indeed, one need not go back too far into Japanese history to see religious commitment. It is hard to describe the fervent loyalty exhibited by Japanese soldiers in the early part of the twentieth century and their willingness to "die for the emperor" in anything other than religious terms.

How, then, should one understand the development of the current Japanese religious landscape? Why have religions been relegated primarily to spiritual service industries, lacking the organizational structure and social role they play in other modern industrialized countries? The difference does not appear to be related to a general lack of religiosity, as was evidenced in Table 8.2. What appears, instead, to be the case is that the social role religious organizations play in a great many countries, including the United States and much of Western Europe, is obviated in Japan by secular group affiliations. Thus we have returned to a discussion of small group interactions.

The Japanese Social Structure
and Its Impact on Religion

It is instructive to note that much of the past and present literature in the sociology of religion emphasizes two different benefits associated with religious organizational involvement: intrinsic and social. Intrinsic benefits are derived directly from religious faith. Religious teachings provide the believer with a variety of explanations concerning issues such as the meaning of life, the nature of the supernatural, and the existence of an afterlife, as well as provide moral guidance (Spiro [1966]; Stark and Bainbridge [1985, 1987]).

However, social benefits can also be obtained from religion, since affiliation with a religion typically involves participation in a supportive social network. Social benefits include opportunities to meet and form personal relationships, attend social gatherings, and receive emotional support during times of personal crisis. Furthermore, membership in a religious organization also provides the individual with an important sense of group identity, and a social setting where status can be achieved apart from one's status in secular society. Thus, religious organizations often occupy an important place in the individual's social environment, and past studies conducted primarily in the United States have shown that it is this aspect of religion, more so than the actual theology, that attracts and retains new members (Lofland and Stark [1965]; Stark and Bainbridge [1980]; Sherkat and Wilson [1995]; Miller [1992b]).

Although specific teachings can differ greatly from religion to religion, most teachings provide a conception of the supernatural and an explanation of eschatological issues. Therefore, most religions provide intrinsic rewards for their adherents. This certainly appears to be the case in

Japan. Religions in Japan provide the people with a variety of eschatological teachings and guidance, especially concerning the existence of ancestral spirits and an afterlife. However, religions in Japan do not provide social rewards, at least not to the extent that they do in many other countries. The reason should be obvious. In general, a wide range of social needs that are addressed by religious organizations in the United States and other countries either do not exist or are addressed by secular group affiliation in Japan.

As has been emphasized throughout this book, a prominent feature of the Japanese social structure is the encouragement of group attachments and group loyalty. From preschool on, group involvement is systematically encouraged, and this type of behavior continues in at least one primary group for nearly all Japanese people at least until the age of retirement. The group repays this commitment and loyalty with social and emotional support. For example, workers often socialize with coworkers after hours, live in company housing, vacation with coworkers at company-owned resorts, and even rely on employers for low-interest loans, counseling, and sometimes matchmaking (Miller [1992b]; Vogel [1985]). Thus, as we have seen, commitment to a secular group is often far stronger and more all-encompassing for Japanese than it is for people in other countries. There is little time or need for an additional organizational affiliation.

Another relevant issue discussed in Chapter 3 is that Japanese schools are active in providing moral guidance to their students. In general, schools have a much broader agenda in Japan than in the United States, and are entrusted with socializing children, an important part of which is moral education. Thus, lessons are taught as part of a school curriculum that emphasizes the importance of group membership and loyalty, filial piety, and a sense of national identity. Again, the result is that Japanese families have no need to join a religious group in order to ensure that their child receives a moral education.

These examples show how secular organizations and institutions in Japan provide a variety of social services that are often relegated to religious organizations in the West. In other words, there are differences in the social structure between Japan and the United States and these differences have led to differences in the role of religious organizations in each society. Thus, primary group affiliation appears to not only affect crime, deviance, and overall social order, but also the development of religious organizations. Simply put, Japanese people do not need social rewards from religious organizations, they merely need intrinsic rewards. Social needs are taken care of through the intense affiliation Japanese have in their secular life. And more practically, even for those individuals who do not feel that secular affiliations adequately address their social needs, little time exists outside of those secular commitments to pursue additional group affiliations.

Empirical Support

The above discussion should not be understood to mean that *no* Japanese religious organizations provide social and emotional support, or that *no* Japanese people are in need of social and emotional support. It is merely the case that, in general, a smaller percentage of religious organizations provide social rewards and a smaller percentage of the Japanese population desire this service from religious organizations. We can therefore conduct some preliminary tests of this thesis by looking at the relationship between social rewards provided by secular organizations and the desire for social rewards from religious organizations. Put simply, most Japanese receive social rewards through occupational affiliations. Even for women who do not work, social and emotional support is often provided by their husband's colleagues, supervisors, and their families (Brinton [1989]; Nakane [1970]). Although these statements represent somewhat of an overgeneralization, it is clearly the case that Japanese workers spend a great deal of time, both professionally and socially, with their coworkers. If it is true that occupational affiliation provides an important source of social rewards, then people who lack these affiliations in Japan are more likely than those with full-time jobs to turn to religious organizations for this support. (Note that past research suggests this relationship is not true in the United States. Even people very committed and involved in their work still desire religious organizational involvement.)

Table 8.3 tests this relationship. Using data from a 1980 survey conducted by the Institute of Statistical Mathematics in Tokyo, we analyze the relationship between religious organizational participation and job involvement. The first column focuses on whether the respondent regularly visits a Buddhist temple or Shinto shrine. The second column focuses on individuals who claim to have faith in a specific religious organization. Logistic regression is used to better understand the patterns, controlling for other characteristics that might influence religious affiliation (i.e., age, marital status, educational attainment, and sex). Coefficients with an asterisk are significantly related to the likelihood that a person will visit a temple regularly or claim to have faith in a religion. What we are interested in testing is the relationship between job involvement and these measures of individual religiosity. Therefore, we construct a somewhat crude measure of job involvement. This measure divides the respondents into those who have the types of occupations typically associated with a strong social involvement with coworkers (e.g., professionals or white-collar workers who work full time in fairly

TABLE 8.3   The Relationship Between Job Involvement and Religiosity

	Attendance	*Affiliation*
Job Involvement	−.54**	−.44*
Age	.03**	.05***
Marital Status	−.33	−.50
Education	−.00	.18
Sex (male = 1)	−.32**	−.01

*p < .05
**p < .01
***p < .001
SOURCE: Committee for the Comparative Survey of Values, Tokyo (1980).

large companies) and respondents who likely do not have strong social involvement at work (e.g., self-employed, unemployed, part-time workers, and so on).

As can be seen in columns one and two of Table 8.3, job involvement is strongly related to both measures of religiosity. The negative sign in front of the coefficient means that people who have strong social involvement with coworkers are far less likely than others to visit temples or be affiliated with a religious organization (even after removing the effects of differences based on age, marital status, education, and sex). The actual coefficients are hard to interpret, but they can be transformed into a form that indicates the increase or decrease in the likelihood of visiting a temple regularly or being affiliated with a religious organization. In the table above, the results indicate that people involved with coworkers exhibit about a 50 percent decrease in the likelihood that they will participate in either of the religious activities under consideration.

In addition, results indicate that older people and females exhibit an increased likelihood of participating in religious organizations. This is consistent with past research on religion in general that show females to be consistently more religious than males (Miller and Hoffmann [1995]) and older people more religious than younger people (Sasaki and Suzuki [1987]). The reason typically cited for these differences is that females' social role as caregivers naturally involves them more in religious activities, and older people, sensing their own mortality, tend to develop an increased interest in religion. However, it is also interesting to note that in general older people and females have weaker social support networks and more free time. Thus, even without care-taking responsibilities and concern over one's own death, these two social groups could be expected to exhibit higher levels of personal religiosity.

We can perform one more test to explore the relationship between secular group affiliations and religiosity. It involves focusing on what are known in Japan as the "New Religions." These religious organizations tend to be similar to sectarian groups in the West and specialize in providing a variety of social rewards (see Miller [1992b]; Earhart [1970]; McFarland [1970]). They are schismatic movements, derived primarily from Buddhism, that began in the latter part of the nineteenth century and have become increasingly popular since World War II (Earhart [1982]; Hardacre [1984]). In general, they emphasize a return to traditional family values, moral education, and this-worldly benefits (Hardacre [1984, 1986]; Kitagawa [1987]). It has been estimated that about 20 percent of the Japanese population is involved in these groups, and adherents tend to exhibit relatively high levels of personal religiosity (Morioka [1975a]). Unlike conventional religious organizations in Japan, New Religions tend to be membership-based and the adherents meet regularly for both social and spiritual activities. Therefore, they demand more from their adherents than mere nominal affiliation, and in return they are able to offer a variety of social rewards (Miller [1992b, 1998]).

Since these organizations tend to require more of a personal commitment, and in exchange offer greater social rewards than are available through conventional religions, one can test whether or not individuals who lack social support in their secular lives are disproportionately drawn to New Religions. Table 8.4 addresses this issue. This table addresses the relationship between social support and affiliation with a New Religion. To this end we construct a more complex measure of overall social support. It uses information related to the individual's occupation, marital status, and education level to produce a scale that runs from 1 to 5, 1 meaning the respondent has a very low level of social support and 5 meaning the respondent has a high level of social support. Therefore, a respondent coded as 1 is likely to be an unskilled laborer who is not married and poorly educated. A respondent coded as 5 is likely to be a professional or skilled white-collar worker who is married and college educated (see Miller [1992b] for a more complete explanation of how this variable was constructed). Note that the reason educational level is significant is that it is the large corporations that provide the most comprehensive forms of social support for their employees, and they hire almost exclusively college graduates.

Once again we used logistic regression, and included age and sex as control variables in the equation.

Again one can see a strong relationship between secular social support and religiosity. The negative coefficient means that people who receive social rewards through secular sources are far less likely than others to join a New Religion.

TABLE 8.4   The Relationship Between Social Support and Affiliation in New
Religions

	Membership: *New Religion*
Social Support	-.41***
Age	.01
Sex (male = 1)	-.06

*p < .05
**p < .01
***p < .001
SOURCE: A Survey of Customs and Traditions, Tokyo: Institute of Statistical
Mathematics (Hayashi, Akuto, and Hayashi 1997).

Conclusion

We have seen throughout this book the all-encompassing nature of primary group membership and how it leads to behavioral conformity and
ultimately to low crime and high social order. Less intuitive is its relationship to religiosity. Because modern Japanese society promotes strong
group dependence throughout school and work life, the social role of religion is obviated. Consider the wide range of social services typically
provided to Americans by religious organizations: a place to make
friends and meet potential spouses, a place to receive counseling and
other forms of general emotional support, a familylike setting to enjoy a
wide variety of social activities, and a safe place to bring children where
they can receive a good moral education. Past studies consistently show
the importance of these services to Americans (Stark and Bainbridge
[1985, 1987]; Miller [1998]; Sherkat and Wilson [1995]; Lofland and Stark
[1965]; Glock, Ringer, and Babbie [1967]). Yet these services are rendered
largely unnecessary because of the nature of social groups in Japan. In return for exclusive commitment and loyalty to a primary group, many, if
not most, Japanese people receive social benefits commensurate with
those provided by religious organizations in the United States.

Of course, not all people receive social and emotional support from
these secular sources. Thus New Religions fill an important social niche.
Although there are fewer Japanese than Americans who look to religious
organizations for social rewards, those who do appear to find that support in New Religions. It is worth noting that New Religions boomed
during two specific historical periods: just after the Meiji Restoration
(1868), and following World War II (McFarland [1970]; Yinger [1970]).
The first was a period of rapid social change, when Japanese society was

being transformed from a feudal to a modern society. This change involved rapid urbanization and industrialization. During such a period, traditional social support networks become less effective. As people abandoned rural farm life and moved to urban centers, a great many were likely in need of establishing new social support networks. Thus the rise of New Religions. Of course, World War II also produced a period of widespread unemployment and a breakdown in various social support networks. Thus the second rise of New Religions took place. In addition, there is currently speculation that a third boom in New Religions has begun, which is sometimes referred to as the "New New Religions" (Numata [1995]). This also comes at a time when the Japanese economy is in deep recession, with unemployment rates rising and lifetime employment opportunities declining. Still, modern Japan has relatively little time or need for voluntary membership organizations. Even during times of intense social upheaval, the majority of people did not join a New Religion.

In conclusion, what we are witnessing in modern Japanese society is a social structure that promotes group dependence and behavioral conformity to the extent that many areas of social life are affected. The fact that religious organizations are forced to specialize in providing spiritual services rather than exist as full-blown membership organizations has had a dramatic effect on the religious life of the Japanese people. If, for example, one were to remove the membership element of Christianity, it might look very different after a few generations. Even if beliefs continued to be strong, behavior would likely change significantly. Without the ability to assemble regularly, one would expect less behavioral commitment and less specific knowledge of the theology. In short, over time it might look more and more like religion does in Japan.

9

Trust

Like religion, trust represents another area where the consequences of the Japanese social structure are both unintentional and non-intuitive. A variety of empirical studies over the last ten years consistently show that Japanese are much less trusting of others than are Americans or Europeans. These results appear to be counterintuitive. After all, Japanese live in a very safe, group-oriented society whereas Americans live in a much more individualistic and often risky society. Shouldn't Americans be very cautious of others and Japanese trusting? To better understand the issues involved in this area of research, it is useful to trace the evolution of the empirical work of Toshio Yamagishi, a leader in this field of study.

Are Japanese Group-Oriented?

When Yamagishi was a faculty member of the sociology department at the University of Washington, he was interested in exploring stereotypical characteristics of Japanese and American societies to see how many could stand up to empirical testing. One of his earliest social psychological experiments tested the notion that Japanese are group-oriented and Americans are individualistic. After all, one can hardly open a book on Japan or America and not find a large section dedicated to these concepts. It is unclear what exactly is meant by the terms "group-oriented" or "individualistic," but they seem to go beyond the issues raised in this book. This book discusses aspects of the Japanese social structure that encourage group identity and dependence. However, discussions of Japan as a "collectivist" society and the Japanese as "group-oriented" seem to imply more than just the effects of the current social environment. They seem to imply a long cultural tradition that is so ingrained in the society that social institutions reflect this orientation rather than produce it. A collectivist culture is typically defined as a culture where group interest is placed ahead of individual interest (e.g., Triandis [1995, 1994]) so that, for example, workers are seen as dedicating themselves to their company not because they are forced to, but because they voluntarily place the company's interest above their own.

Yamagishi, of course, knew that the modern Japanese social structure left individuals little choice but to participate in groups. He wondered what would happen if that structure were removed. Would Japanese people still prefer to act in groups, especially when compared to their American counterparts? The design of the experiment was fairly simple. Using American and Japanese subjects, Yamagishi (1988a) designed an experimental situation where subjects were initially assigned to groups and given simple tasks to perform, with a monetary reward being distributed evenly among the group members at the completion of each task. Also, after the completion of each task, subjects were given the choice of continuing to work in groups or opt to work individually. Subjects who chose to work individually were rewarded based on their own performance, whereas those who stayed in the group were rewarded based on the performance of the group. However, the amount of money awarded for completing a task was less if the subject chose to work individually. In other words, the subjects were typically better off staying in the group.

Readers not familiar with this type of research might not be familiar with the concept of "free riders." Free riders are those individuals who do not contribute adequately to the group but still enjoy the rewards of group membership. In the case of this experiment, it means that people who did not contribute at all, or who did not perform well, would still receive a reward identical to that received by other group members. The research question, then, can be thought of as involving tolerance of free riders. Who would be more likely to resent the free riders (either because they brought down the level of the group's performance or because they were being rewarded even though they were not contributing their fair share)? Would the American subjects choose to leave the group and work individually? Would the Japanese subjects prefer to stay in the group?

Intuitively, two outcomes seemed plausible. The Japanese subjects might prefer to work in groups, even if there were some free riders. After all, the Japanese subjects were raised in a "collectivist" culture where they were accustomed to working in groups. They have been socialized to appreciate the value of cooperation, and therefore, might feel more comfortable being evaluated as a group member rather than as an individual, especially given that the reward structure favored group loyalty. Such an outcome would be consistent with much of the literature on Japan. However, it was also possible that behavior, whether it be in Japan or the United States, is determined primarily by the social structure. Since both the Japanese and American subjects were operating under the same structural characteristics, they might respond similarly (regardless of what that response might be). The results, however, did not follow either of these intuitive predictions. The Japanese participants were actually *less* likely than their American counterparts to continue working in groups. American subjects chose to exit the group in only slightly more than one out of twenty trials, whereas their Japanese counterparts exited the group in about eight out of twenty trials, even though it meant losing money.

What could explain these counterintuitive findings? If Japanese people prefer to be part of a group whereas Americans value independence, the results should have been different. Yamagishi explained these counterintuitive findings in terms of tolerance for free riders. As this book has demonstrated, Japanese groups have efficient monitoring and sanctioning systems, which greatly reduces the number of free riders. Everyone must contribute to the group or face harsh sanctioning. In Yamagishi's experiment, however, monitoring and sanctioning of other group participants was not possible. He therefore concluded that the Japanese subjects were unaccustomed to, and uncomfortable with, this type of group and were more likely than their American counterparts to opt out.

Based on these initial findings, Yamagishi and his colleagues began exploring in more depth the nature of group affiliation in Japan. Although Japanese often work in groups, those groups have certain characteristics. They tend to be fixed and long-term, where all members share a high dependency on the group, and high visibility allows for constant monitoring and sanctioning of inappropriate behavior. Japanese are not accustomed to forming *temporary groups* composed of strangers or loose acquaintances, whose behavior cannot be controlled by the group. Americans are far more likely than Japanese to meet a person or a group of people and form a short-term alliance in order to perform a given task. Therefore, the relevant issue in Yamagishi's study turned out *not* to be whether people are "group-oriented" or "individualistic," but rather how comfortable they were performing short-term tasks with people whom they do not know well and could not monitor and sanction. This realization led to a new line of research concerning the ability to meet and work with people outside of one's group.

Generalized Trust

Based on the above results, Yamagishi and his colleagues proposed that Japanese people will have lower levels of "generalized trust" than do Americans. Generalized trust refers to an "expectation of goodwill and benign intent" (Yamagishi and Yamagishi [1994, 131]). It is the belief that someone will act fairly even when it might be to their advantage not to do so. Indeed, when one thinks about it, trust is really only possible when a person actually *can* be cheated. In other words, trust can only occur when a person is in a vulnerable position. Otherwise, there is no need for trust. Yamagishi and Yamagishi refer to a situation where a person cannot be cheated as entailing "assurance" rather than trust. This distinction makes good sense since it is obvious that a person need not "trust" another person when that person has no choice but to act fairly. For example, if one purchases a winning lottery ticket, there is no need to "trust" that the lottery officials will honor the ticket. Laws require that they do, so one is assured of not being cheated. However, if one asks a friend to purchase a ticket and it turns out to be the winning ticket, believing that your friend will hand over the ticket involves trust.

This distinction seems particularly relevant when discussing the Japanese social structure and the nature of group affiliations. Consistent with the arguments presented in this book, Yamagishi and his colleagues note that Japanese live and work in group settings where long-term affiliation is assumed, and monitoring and sanctioning inappropriate behavior is maintained. In short, Japanese are accustomed to a high-assurance environment where there is little risk of being cheated (Yamagishi [1988a, 1988b]; Yamagishi and Yamagishi [1994]; Hechter and Kanazawa [1993]). As this book illustrates, high dependence on the group and high visibility in one's daily life allows the group to demand and enforce behavioral conformity. Since these behavioral expectations apply to all group members, and most people live much of their lives within this semiclosed environment, there is little chance of being cheated either by other group members or by people outside of the group. Technically speaking, then, trust is not necessary. Individuals are *assured* by the very nature of their social environment that others will behave in a predictable and responsible way.

This distinction between trust and assurance is routinely misunderstood. For example, in an otherwise excellent book, Rohlen (1974) discusses how the strong sense of belonging among employees and a closed social network "produces great trust" when dealing with other members within the same company (15). Similarly, Kumon (1992) states that "information sharing and consensus formation in networks can only take place effectively when based on long-standing and stable relations of mutual trust. And, conversely when a network functions effectively, mutual trust among its members will be reinforced" (136). In both cases, it is clear that the authors are discussing assurance rather than trust. An impressive amount of social psychological literature has studied the formation of long-term, stable relations as a risk-reducing strategy (DiMaggio and Louch [1998]; Kollock [1994]; Yamagishi et al. [1995]; Cook and Emerson [1978]). In such situations, it is not trust (i.e., a belief in the benign intentions of others), per se, that serves to reduce the risk of uncertainty. Rather, it is assurance, since all members have a vested interest in maintaining the relationship.

It is instructive to note here that Francis Fukuyama, in his highly influential book *Trust: The Social Virtues and Creation of Prosperity* (1995), appears to contradict the work of Yamagishi and his colleagues when he describes Japanese society as high in trust. However, a careful reading of Fukuyama's book suggests that his use of the word "trust" is basically analogous to Yamagishi's use of the word "assurance." He does not use the word "trust" to suggest that Japanese people have a generalized trust in the benign intentions of others, but rather to describe "safe environments." That is, he claims that Japanese can "trust" one another because they are in a social environment where there are structural guarantees that they will not be taken advantage of (i.e., "high assurance environments" in the language adopted by Yamagishi et al.).

Is this distinction between trust and assurance merely a difference in semantics? According to Yamagishi and his colleagues, it is definitely not. Rather, it has far-reaching and important social consequences. The reason is that living in a closed social environment dominated by long-term relations does not merely mean assurance that other members will adhere to the group's normative expectations. It also means there is no reason to trust people outside of one's group. Thus, "assurance" is not only a more accurate term to describe what we normally call "trust of in-group members," it is also, in a sense, the antithesis of generalized trust. That is, since Japanese people spend much of their time in tight-knit groups characterized by long-term relations in a setting where they can monitor and sanction other members for inappropriate behavior, there is no reason to develop a sense of generalized trust (i.e., a belief that one can trust a stranger to act in a benign fashion even when it is to his or her advantage not to do so). A wide range of social scientific research supports this contention (Kiyonari and Yamagishi [1996]). After all, if one is always in a closed and safe environment, why would one need to develop trust in the benign intentions of strangers?

A variety of studies have confirmed that Japanese have low levels of generalized trust, especially when compared to Americans. One of the earliest studies was a survey conducted by the Institute of Statistical Mathematics (Hayashi et al. [1982]). Using nationally representative samples in both Japan and the United States, they found that 47 percent of Americans said that in general "people can be trusted," while only 26 percent of Japanese gave this response. Similarly, about 47 percent of Americans said that in general "people try to be helpful," whereas only 19 percent of Japanese chose this response.

More systemically, Yamagishi and Yamagishi (1994) conducted a detailed survey of generalized trust in Japan and the United States. Results are reproduced in Table 9.1. The numbers represent mean responses to the statements on the left. Respondents could choose from a five-point scale (with 1 indicating disagreement and 5 indicating agreement). Thus, the higher the score, the higher the level of generalized trust. The last column shows t-scores. Those t-scores with asterisks indicate that the difference in the mean scores obtained in Japan and the United States are statistically significant.

With the exception of the last question, Japanese respondents consistently exhibited significantly lower levels of generalized trust than their American counterparts. Social psychological experiments conducted with both American and Japanese subjects have yielded similar results (Yamagishi [1998]; Yamagishi [1988b]).

Are these differences important? Since living in a high-assurance environment obviates the need for generalized trust, why would its absence be of any social importance? Just as high social order has both its positive and negative social consequences, so does living in a high-assurance environment. Although risk is reduced, so are opportunities. In economic terms, one can say that living in a high-assurance environment reduces transaction costs but imposes opportunity costs. Or in more simple terms, the cost of maintaining a long-term, low-risk relationship is that one is unable to explore opportunities that exist outside the relationship. To the extent that outside opportunities are limited or very risky, staying in a closed, long-term relationship would seem to be a good strategy. For the most part, this has been the case in Japan. The social structure, by encouraging group affiliation, also reduces opportunity costs. It does this by punishing, rather than rewarding, changing groups. In Japan, loyalty to the group and seniority within the group are rewarded. Therefore, there are few opportunities outside of established relations.

However, even if opportunity costs were to rise in Japan and it would be to the person's advantage to abandon one group for another, studies suggest that Japanese people would be reluctant to do so. The reason is related to generalized trust. A great deal of social psychological research has shown that people with high generalized trust are more willing than people with low trust to leave one relationship in pursuit of better opportunities elsewhere; conversely, people with low generalized trust tend to stay in a relationship even when better outside opportunities exist (Yamagishi and Yamagishi [1994]). Since many Japanese tend to live in closed, high-assurance environments, they do not develop generalized trust. The result is that they prefer the security provided by the committed relationship to potential rewards available elsewhere. As the world, and especially world economies, become more and more global, opportunity costs will likely rise, and the cost of remaining in closed, long-term relations will also rise.

TABLE 9.1   A Japan–U.S. Comparison of Generalized Trust

Item	Japan	United States	T-Score
1. Most people are basically honest.	3.29 (1.34)	3.72 (1.10)	6.52***
2. Most people are basically good and kind.	3.36 (1.19)	3.71 (0.99)	5.93***
3. Most people are trustworthy.	2.64 (1.22)	3.56 (1.06)	14.84***
4. Most people respond in kind when they are trusted by others.	3.51 (1.21)	4.22 (0.73)	14.20***
5. I am trustful.	3.74 (1.10)	4.43 (0.89)	13.02***
6. Most people are trustful of others.	2.96 (1.12)	3.17 (1.07)	3.50***
7. Trusting others will more often result in a happy rather than tragic ending.	3.09 (1.17)	3.18 (1.18)	1.36

NOTE: Standard deviations are in parentheses.
*p < .05
**p < .01
***p < .001
SOURCE: Yamagishi and Yamagishi (1994), T-scores did not appear in the original.

For better or worse, opportunity costs have always been high in the United States. A person who does not pursue outside opportunities as they arise tends to lose out in the long run. Because American society is fairly fluid, with people forming new relationships and changing group affiliations regularly, generalized trust tends to be high. It is an adaptive strategy to deal with a social environment where contact with strangers and short-term relationships often lead to new opportunities and higher rewards. Thus, Americans appear to be better suited for living in a global marketplace where, to remain competitive, one must constantly search for better products, prices, suppliers, new clients, and so on.

Of course, not all Japanese live in closed environments and have low levels of generalized trust, nor do all Americans live in open environments and have high levels of generalized trust. The above example is merely a broad characterization of the two countries. Indeed, it might be interesting to see if Americans who live in fairly closed, high-assurance environments also have relatively low levels of generalized trust. It is difficult to find examples of this, since in general Americans are not highly dependent and committed to one specific group. However, we can conduct some tentative tests of this hypothesis. In Chapter 3 it was proposed that a tight-knit church community might be somewhat analogous to group life in Japan, since it is a fairly closed social environment with strong normative obligations and high visibility. In short, it is an environment characterized by high assurance. A person will not likely be cheated by other church members since that might affect that person's reputation and standing within the church.

Of course, it is difficult to know how closed an environment actually is. In order for people to not develop high levels of generalized trust, they must not only be members of a group characterized by high assurance, but they should also have fairly limited contact with people outside of that group. One rough way of testing for this relationship is to look at differences in generalized trust between religious denominations. Specifically, studies of religious denominations in the United States show that fundamentalist Christian denominations are characterized by fairly tight-knit social networks (Stark and Bainbridge [1980, 1987]; Sherkat and Wilson [1995]; Miller [1992b]). These types of denominations often require a strong commitment in terms of time, as well as specific behavioral expectations, and in return offer a very supportive environment. Although fundamentalist Christians are unlikely to spend as much time in their groups as Japanese spend in theirs, and are likely to have jobs that require them to interact with people outside of their group, their social environment is probably more closed than other Americans' social environment, and their friendship network probably has higher levels of assurance against mistreatment than do other Americans' networks. Therefore, using data from the American General Social Survey (Davis and Smith [1996]), we compare levels of generalized trust between people who are affiliated with fundamentalist Christian denominations, those who are affiliated with moderate denominations, and those who are affiliated with liberal denominations.

Results are presented in Tables 9.2a, 9.2b, and 9.2c. Three different questions were asked. The first asked respondents if they believe that in general most people can be trusted. The second question asks if most people try to be fair, or if given the chance they will take advantage of you. The third question asks whether most of the time people try to be helpful or if they just look out for themselves.

The pattern that appears in these tables clearly supports the theoretical argument advanced by Yamagishi and his colleagues. The more tight-knit the denomination, the lower the levels of generalized trust. Like Yamagishi's study of Japan, these results have a counterintuitive element to them. Fundamentalist Christians typically live in a very close, supportive social environment, where they can expect to be treated fairly by

TABLE 9.2a   Belief that People Are Trustworthy by Religious Denomination

Denomination	Can Trust	Cannot Trust
Fundamentalist	31%	69%
Moderate	46%	54%
Liberal	50%	50%

TABLE 9.2b   Belief that People Are Fair by Religious Denomination

Denomination	Fair	Take Advantage
Fundamentalist	53%	47%
Moderate	66%	34%
Liberal	67%	33%

TABLE 9.2c   Belief that People Are Helpful by Religious Denomination

Denomination	Helpful	Out for Themselves
Fundamentalist	46%	54%
Moderate	56%	44%
Liberal	58%	42%

SOURCE: American General Social Survey (1972–1996).

their friends and helped during times of need. Thus, one might expect that fundamentalist Christians would develop a very positive view of other people's trustworthiness and helpfulness. Clearly this is not the case. Rather, because their friendship network is composed primarily of other church members, there is no need to trust outsiders. The pattern is the same as the one observed in Japan.

Before ending this discussion of generalized trust, it is interesting to note that high generalized trust does not necessarily mean high vulnerability. In a fascinating study of gullibility, Kikuchi, Watanabe, and Yamagishi (1997) tested how accurately respondents are able to predict a person's trustworthiness. In a controlled experiment, subjects were allowed to talk together for thirty minutes before participating in a type of Prisoner's Dilemma game where a person's playing partner, if he or she chose, could try to cheat him or her. Respondents with high generalized trust were able to discern their partner's trustworthiness (i.e., guess whether or not their playing partner would try to cheat them) with 69 percent accuracy. Low trusters achieved only a 43 percent accuracy rate. Kikuchi and her colleagues hypothesized that people who have high generalized trust develop social skills that allow them to more accurately gauge the trustworthiness of strangers. Thus, it would appear that Americans not only have higher levels of generalized trust than Japanese, but are also better able to assess the trustworthiness of strangers, thus reducing some of the risk involved in forming new relationships.

Redefining a Culture of Collectivism

Research in this field implies that not only is the term "trust" often misunderstood and misused, but also the concept of a "collectivist culture" is misleading, since it is not the culture, per se, that is "collectivist." Instead, it is groups within a collectivist culture that are collectivist in nature. It is not that people put the interests of others within their shared culture above their own interests. Rather, they put the interests of those within a specific group above their own interests. This is quite a bit different from what we normally think of as the defining characteristics of a collectivist culture.

Given this difference, we can reformulate what a collectivist culture actually is. Based on the above research, we propose that a collectivist culture exists when there is an adaptive advantage to maintaining close in-group ties. That is, collectivist cultures are sustained by an environment in which opportunity costs are low, and loyalty to one's group pays in the long run. Yamagishi, Jin, and Miller (1998) state that "the defining feature of collectivism is the group heuristic or expectation of generalized reciprocity among, but not extending beyond, members of the same group." In other words, collectivism refers to stable, long-term group affiliations characterized by reciprocal exchanges so that over the long run, one's loyalty and commitment to the group is to one's advantage. Much of this book has shown how the Japanese social structure promotes the formation of these types of groups. Long-term group affiliations are necessary in order to achieve success in many areas of Japanese society. Furthermore, seniority within the group, loyalty to other group members, and sacrifice for the good of the group, all characteristics associated with collectivism, are rational behavioral decisions in the context of Japanese society. Since group affiliations are long-term, dependence on the group is high, and changing groups is difficult and costly, being a good group member is the best strategy available. This is, of course, a very different perspective of collectivist cultures. Rather than claiming that people born into a specific culture come to internalize norms and values that support self-sacrifice, it rather claims that the social structure creates an environment where loyalty to specific groups is a rational adaptive strategy for success.

Consistent with the above discussion, Yamagishi, Jin, and Miller also redefine "individualistic" cultures, which they claim are characterized by more diffuse relations that go beyond the confines of a single, closed group. In other words, if the defining characteristic of a collectivist culture is its strong in-group mentality, the defining characteristic of an individualistic culture is its lack of a strong in-group, out-group distinction. Yamagishi and his colleagues explain the difference this way:

> We use the term "universalistic" instead of the usual term "individualistic" to make a contrast with "collectivist," because we believe that the contrast between collectivism and individualism is based on the premise that the defining feature of collectivism is priority given to group interests as compared to individual interests. If we abandon this feature as the core of collectivism and adopt expectations of generalized reciprocity within group boundaries as the defining feature of collectivism, then the contrast is not between groups and individuals but rather between generalized reciprocity being limited within group boundaries and being diffused beyond boundaries. In other words, how important group boundaries are in estimating behaviors of others lies in the core of collectivism. If people expect totally different behaviors from in-group members than from out-group members, they live in a culture of collectivism. If they expect similar behaviors from in-group and out-group members, then they live in a culture of universalism, not of individualism." (323)

An important implication of this redefinition is that, contrary to prior definitions, individuals in collectivist cultures are no more altruistic toward fellow group members and no less egoistic than individuals in universalistic cultures. If the price of a loaf of bread is the same in the neighborhood store as it is in a store across town (analogous to a universalistic culture), then one would buy bread at either store, and constantly price compare, ready to exhibit a preference should one or the other store offer a better deal. But if the price is always markedly higher in the store across town (analogous to the collectivist culture), then one would buy exclusively from the neighborhood store, and not even bother to price compare since the effort would nearly always be futile. In this analogy, one needs to recognize that the cost of doing business across town is intentionally kept high by the neighborhood store by either punishing or withholding rewards from people who do business with other stores. In other words, people in collectivist cultures are not more altruistic toward one another than people in universalistic cultures. In both cases, people merely behave rationally given the nature of the social environment.

Conclusion

The results of the studies reviewed here concerning trust in Japan are both intuitive and counterintuitive. It makes intuitive sense that when people live in a relatively safe, closed environment, they will be reluctant to develop trust in outsiders. However, there is also a counterintuitive dimension to this discussion. In the United States, with its high crime rate and relatively open, high-risk environment where it is easy to be cheated, one would expect people to be wary of strangers and somewhat cynical concerning their intentions. Alternatively, in Japan where crime is low, there is a shared collectivist culture, and supportive interpersonal relations abound, one might expect high levels of generalized trust and more optimism concerning the benign intentions of others. This is not the case.

The apparent counterintuitive nature of these results likely stems from both a misunderstanding of what the term "trust" means and also a misunderstanding of what a collectivist culture actually is. Trust does not apply to situations where one is secure in the knowledge that one cannot be cheated. That is assurance. Trust entails vulnerability, and the belief that, despite being in a vulnerable position, one will be treated fairly. Most Japanese people, by virtue of living in a high-assurance environment, have no need for trust (i.e., generalized trust). They live much of their lives enmeshed in social networks that both demand and reward their loyalty. And it is this characteristic that is the defining feature of a collectivist culture.

Throughout this book we have described ways in which the Japanese social structure is designed to encourage group affiliations. We also showed how those groups provide environments where monitoring and sanctioning of inappropriate behavior leads to high levels of behavioral conformity. We have further shown how this conformity at the group level leads to a wide range of positive and negative, as well as intuitive and nonintuitive, social consequences. Generalized trust can now be added to this list. Once again, it is clear that there is a price to be paid for living in a highly secure social environment.

There are some ambiguities in the theoretical argument advanced by Yamagishi and his colleagues. They claim that long-term committed relationships produce high-assurance environments that tend to inhibit the development of generalized trust. Without generalized trust, people are unwilling or unable to explore outside opportunities. However, they also claim that it is the existence of outside opportunities (i.e., opportunity costs) that foster the development of generalized trust, since increases in outside opportunities render commitment to a long-term relationship disadvantageous. Of course, there is a problem with this argument since it does not state clearly how, when opportunity costs increase, a person in a high-assurance environment develops enough generalized trust to explore those opportunities.

Nevertheless, despite the incomplete nature of the theoretical argument, it is clear that there is a relationship between the type of all-encompassing group affiliations one sees in Japan and the relatively low levels of generalized trust exhibited by the Japanese. What past researchers often described as "trust" among Japanese is really a sense of security. As long as that security exists, there is no problem. However, once that security is removed, Japanese are ill at ease and distrustful of others. One of Yamagishi's (1988b) experiments graphically displays this concept. When sanctions were in place, Japanese participants cooperated with one another at a high level, higher than their American counterparts. However, once the sanctioning system was removed the Japanese participants were far less cooperative than their American counterparts. With no experience working in open environments where agreements between relative strangers entail generalized trust rather than monitoring and sanctioning, Japanese are ill prepared and ill at ease. This characteristic has likely contributed to some of the negative images other people have had toward Japanese people in the past, and might be increasingly problematic in a world that is growing more and more "universalistic."

PART FOUR

Speculations and Conclusions

10

The Emergence of
Cooperative Social Institutions

In this book we have explained how unique social institutions in Japan, which foster the dependence and visibility of members of various groups (schools, work organizations, and families) increase the solidarity of these groups, and, as their unintended consequence, also produce social order in Japanese society. We have also described how the same social institutions encourage white-collar crime, obviate the need for organized religion, and prevent the development of generalized trust in Japan. Given how pervasive the intended and unintended consequences of these social institutions are, the reader might ask how they came to be in Japan. Why is it that Japan has these unique social institutions?

We attempt to answer this question in two steps. First, we present a theory of the emergence of cooperative social institutions. The unique institutions that foster dependence and visibility in Japanese groups are examples of cooperative social institutions, and thus a general theory of such institutions should be able to account for their emergence in Japan. Then, in the second part of this chapter, we will discuss a set of historical initial conditions that might have led to the emergence of highly effective cooperative social institutions in Japan and nowhere else in the world (at least not to the same extent). But first we will begin with a brief discussion of cooperative social institutions.

What Are Cooperative Social Institutions?

A cooperative social institution is a set of rules that prescribe individuals to behave in ways that benefit other members of a group or the group as a whole at the cost of individuals' self-interest (Hechter [1990]). These rules are necessary when there is a conflict of interest between individuals and groups, when what benefits the individuals does not necessarily benefit the group, and vice versa. When there is no such conflict, cooperative social institutions are not necessary.

A brief discussion of the Prisoner's Dilemma game might be useful to illuminate the concept of cooperative social institution. Figure 10.1 presents a payoff matrix of a typical Prisoner's Dilemma game. The matrix, with these particular numbers, is carefully constructed to create a situation where individual self-interest leads to collective disaster. (The numbers do not necessarily have to be the particular ones we have chosen in this illustration, but they do have to satisfy certain mathematical requirements.) Prisoner's Dilemma and other related games have been used to analyze these situations for the past half-century, because they capture important aspects of real-life situations that concern social theorists (Kollock [1998]).

There are two players in this game (A and B), each of whom can make one of two choices: cooperate or defect. The two players make their decisions on their own, without consultation with each other, and players cannot influence each other's decision. The numbers inside each cell in Figure 10.1 represent the payoffs each player receives out of a given joint outcome. The first number in each cell represents the payoff to Player A, the second number the payoff to Player B. For instance, if Player A cooperates and Player B defects, then Player A receives –10 points and Player B receives 10 points. There are four possible joint outcomes.

It is apparent that, left to themselves, players will choose to defect, because doing so will always bring larger payoffs regardless of what the other player chooses. For instance, from Player A's perspective, there are two possible states of the world: 1) Player B cooperates; or 2) Player B defects. Player A must make a decision in complete ignorance of which state of the world prevails. In the fist state of the world, Player A can either cooperate and receive 5 points, or defect and receive 10 points. Player A is better off defecting in this state of the world. In the second state of the world (in which Player B defects), Player A can either cooperate and receive –10 points, or defect and receive –5 points. Player A is better off defecting in this state of the world. Player A is better off defecting in either state of the world. And since the payoff matrix is symmetrical, the situation is identical for Player B. Thus both players are better off defecting, and, left to themselves, will choose to do so.

However, the joint outcome of the two decisions (–5, –5) is not as good as if both players decided to cooperate (5, 5). As a group, the first joint outcome produces –10, whereas the second joint outcome produces 10. The group is much better off if individuals cooperated than if they defected, even though it is individually rational to defect (because defection leads to a larger payoff in either state of the world). Hence the dilemma: Individually rational behavior, if everyone chooses it, leads to a collective

Player B

	Cooperate	Defect
Cooperate	5, 5	−10, 10
Defect	10, −10	−5, −5

Player A

FIGURE 10.1   Payoff Matrix of Prisoner's Dilemma

disaster. Although our example uses a two-person game, the essence of the game is easily generalizable to a greater number of players. The Prisoner's Dilemma game is one instance of a large class of phenomena called social dilemmas, in which individually rational decisions lead to a collectively irrational and disastrous situation (Kollock [1998]). In Prisoner's Dilemma games (as well as in other social dilemmas), it is individually rational to defect, but the collective outcome is a disaster if everybody behaved rationally. Social dilemmas encompass a large class of real-life phenomena, from contribution to public radio stations to recycling to air pollution.

Think of the presidential elections in the United States, for example. In a typical presidential election, millions of voters cast their ballots, and the election is decided by a margin of at least tens of thousands of votes (usually many more). Thus, a person's one vote makes absolutely no difference to the electoral outcome. His or her favorite candidate either wins or loses the election whether or not that person votes. Furthermore, voting involves a cost. A person must use his or her personal time and energy, even though there is no chance that the single vote will influence the election results.

This example is roughly analogous to the Prisoner's Dilemma game decision matrix. There are two possible outcomes: The person's candidate will either win or lose the election. But in either case, the rational strategy is not to vote since the cost of voting will always exceed the pay-off. Thus, an individual should always choose to defect (i.e., not vote). However, as with the Prisoner's Dilemma game, if everyone acted ratio-nally, the result would be very costly for everyone, much more costly than if every person chose the opposite strategy. This is obvious since if everyone acted in their own self-interest, no one would vote and the democracy would collapse (which nobody wants). Thus, the total col-lapse of democracy is the collective disaster to which individually ratio-nal decisions lead.

Because the cooperative choice (such as voting) benefits the other player(s) and the group as a whole, even though it is costly for any indi-vidual to cooperate (because each player forgoes a larger payoff by coop-erating), any social institution (a set of norms) that dictates that individu-als cooperate rather than defect is an example of a cooperative social institution. (Democratic institutions that prescribe voting are therefore cooperative institutions.) In the absence of such institutions, we expect all individuals to choose to defect and a collective disaster to ensue. If people need to avoid such collective disasters, if they want to increase the solidarity of the group (by making sure that group members cooperate), then they need cooperative social institutions.

How Do Cooperative Social Institutions Emerge?

The emergence of cooperative social institutions is a formidable theoreti-cal problem precisely because it dictates that individuals behave in an in-dividually irrational (albeit collectively rational) manner. How can such institutions emerge?

There are two distinct approaches to the explanation of the origin of in-stitutions (Hechter [1990, 15]; Kanazawa and Still [1999]). Institutions can be imposed on society *top-down* by its political leaders or they can spon-taneously emerge *bottom-up* from the aggregation of individual behavior. Because cooperative social institutions dictate that individuals behave in ways that hurt their self-interest, their emergence bottom-up is theoreti-cally more challenging than their emergence top-down. It is not difficult to explain how social institutions that benefit groups and society can emerge if one assumes the existence of political leaders who can impose institutions on the individuals (because the political leaders might very well benefit personally from such social institutions). Given the wide-spread existence of cooperative institutions, however, it is clear that not all emerge because they are imposed by political leaders top-down. Therefore, we will attempt to explain the emergence of cooperative social institutions without assuming the existence of political leaders.

In order to explain the spontaneous emergence of cooperative social institutions, one must begin with the state of nature. This is the state that assumes the prior existence of nothing, except for self-interested individuals. There are no laws, no police, and no government. In the state of nature, individuals behave as they wish, completely unconstrained by institutions. Under such conditions, individual behavior can vary: Some people do X, other people do Y. It is the fundamental assumption of the bottom-up theory of institutional emergence that the institution prescribing X emerges when many or most people already do X in the absence of any rules regarding such behavior (Homans [1950, 265–268]; Knight [1992]; Kanazawa and Still [1999]). If most people do Y, then the emergent institution would prescribe Y.

In the state of nature, neither X nor Y is normative; neither is prescribed nor proscribed. Neither carries any moral or social significance. Under such conditions, it is reasonable to assume that an institution prescribing the more common behavior might emerge, purely as a matter of statistical expectation (Knight [1992]). Once the institution is in place, however, it will have a further effect on individual behavior. If the emergent institution dictates X, then those who were inclined to do Y before are now forced to do X (in order to avoid the negative sanctions) and those who mostly but not always did X are now required to do X all the time (for the same reason).

It therefore follows that cooperative social institutions, which dictate cooperation and altruism, emerge when many or most people already cooperate and behave altruistically. The evolution of cooperation is a tremendous theoretical problem because cooperation is individually irrational and maladaptive. As the payoffs in Figure 10.1 show, defection is always an individually rational strategy. In the language of evolutionary biology, defectors have higher fitness, in the sense that they (and their offspring) will do better than cooperators (and their offspring). Unless cooperators change their ways and start defecting, they will soon be wiped out by defectors, who thrive at the cost of cooperators. How then can cooperation emerge? How can cooperators survive and outperform defectors when the latter have higher fitness than the former?

This question was once considered "the central theoretical problem of sociobiology" (Wilson [1980, 3]). A recent theory called multilevel selection theory (Sober and Wilson [1998]) offers a novel and very promising solution to this formidable problem. Sober and Wilson propose one way to solve "the central theoretical problem of sociobiology" by reintroducing a sophisticated version of group selection into evolutionary theory. Since cooperative social institutions are assumed to emerge when most people already cooperate in the absence of such institutions, the theoretical problem has the same solution as "the central theoretical problem of sociobiology." How does cooperation evolve?

Assume a society that consists of 200 individuals (Figure 10.2). One hundred of these people are cooperators, and thus the proportion of co-operators in this society is .500. The 200 individuals in this society belong to two groups: Group 1, with twenty cooperators and eighty defectors; and Group 2, with eighty cooperators and twenty defectors. Thus Group 2 has far more cooperators than Group 1. Members of each group only in-teract with other members of the same group. This is how this hypotheti-cal society looks at the beginning of our observation (Generation 1).

By definition, defectors do better than cooperators *within each group*, and they leave a larger number of offspring on average than cooperators. In Group 1, for instance, cooperators leave 9.96 offspring on average, whereas defectors leave 11.01 offspring on average.[1] Defectors clearly outperform cooperators. As a result, the proportion of cooperators in Group 1 declines slightly at the end of our observation (Generation 2). Group 1 now consists of 1,080 individuals, only 199 (20 * 9.96) of whom are cooperators and the other 881 (80 * 11.01) of whom are defectors. The proportion of cooperators in Group 1 declines slightly (from .200 to .184).

The situation is essentially the same for Group 2. Within this group, as in Group 1, defectors outperform cooperators and leave a larger number of offspring. In Group 2, cooperators leave 12.99 offspring on average, whereas defectors leave 14.04 offspring on average. As a result, at the end of our observation (in Generation 2), there are 1,320 individuals in Group 2, 1,039 (80 * 12.99) of whom are cooperators and the other 281 (20 * 14.04) of whom are defectors. The proportion of cooperators in Group 2 also de-clines slightly (from .800 to .787).

Although the proportion of cooperators in each group decreases, *their proportion in the global population increases*. At the end of our observation (Generation 2), there are 2,400 individuals in this society, 1,238 (199 + 1,039) of whom are cooperators. The proportion of cooperators in the population increases (from .500 to .516). This is because more cooperative groups (groups that contain more cooperators, such as Group 2) grow faster than less cooperative groups (groups that contain fewer coopera-tors, such as Group 1). Cooperation and altruism by definition benefit the group as a whole, and thus groups grow in direct proportion to the num-

---

[1]The numbers of offspring that cooperators and defectors leave in the two groups are ar-bitrarily chosen (by Sober and Wilson) so that the size of the population in Generation 2 will be a nice round number (2,400). There is no other meaning to these numbers. The only theoretical requirements for these numbers are that defectors leave more offspring than co-operators *within each group* and that the average fitness (across both cooperators and defec-tors) is proportionate to the relative share of cooperators in the group.

Generation 1
Population size = 200
Number of cooperators = 100
Proportion of cooperators = .500

Group 1
Group size = 100
Number of cooperators = 20
Proportion of cooperators = .200

Average number of offspring
Cooperators = 9.96
Defectors = 11.01

Group 1
Group size = 1,080
Number of cooperators = 199
Proportion of cooperators = .184

Group 2
Group size = 100
Number of cooperators = 80
Proportion of cooperators = .800

Average number of offspring
Cooperators = 12.99
Defectors = 14.04

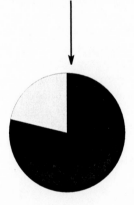

Group 2
Group size = 1,320
Number of cooperators = 1,039
Proportion of cooperators = .787

Generation 2
Population size = 2,400
Number of cooperators = 1,238
Proportion of cooperators = .516

FIGURE 10.2   How Cooperation Evolves Through Multilevel Selection (Sober and Wilson 1998, Figure 1.1)

ber of cooperators in them. Individuals (both cooperators and defectors) in more cooperative groups do better and leave more offspring than individuals (both cooperators and defectors) in less cooperative groups. Through this multilevel selection process, cooperators grow in number at the global population level, whereas they lose ground relative to defectors in each group.

There are four necessary conditions for cooperation to evolve through multilevel selection (Sober and Wilson [1998, 26–30]). First, there must be more than one group in the society; there must be a population of groups. Second, groups must vary in their proportion of cooperators so that some groups are more cooperative than others. Third, there must be a direct relationship between the proportion of cooperators in a group and its level of solidarity; groups with higher proportions of cooperators must "do better" and thrive more than groups with lower proportions of cooperators. Fourth, individuals from different groups must occasionally migrate between groups or form new ones. Otherwise, if the membership in each group is permanent, then cooperation will eventually die down in every group.

None of these conditions is difficult to meet. There are always more than one group in every society (Condition 1). For a hunting and gathering society, for instance, each band can function as a group, not a society, since these bands compete against each other for local resources. The third condition (the direct relationship between the proportion of cooperators and its success) is true by definition. Since cooperation always benefits the group (albeit at a cost to individuals), groups with more cooperators must by definition do better and have higher levels of solidarity. And the principle of homophily, where individuals who are alike are more likely to form a group and associate with each other, can simultaneously satisfy conditions two and four. Through homophily, cooperators are more likely to associate with other cooperators (because they don't want to be taken advantage of by the defectors), and defectors are more likely to associate with other defectors (if not by choice, then because they are shunned by cooperators). This will ensure the heterogeneity of groups, where some groups are more cooperative than others. Homophily will also ensure that cooperators from groups that consist mostly of defectors would want to leave their groups and migrate to others where there are more cooperators. It will also ensure that defectors from groups that consist mostly of cooperators are likely to be expelled from their groups and must form groups of their own.

Through this process of multilevel selection, the average level of cooperation in the global population (as well as the average level of cooperation among the groups after migration and formation of new groups) will gradually increase. More cooperative groups will eventually take over less cooperative groups. When most individuals in each group cooperate anyway, the emergent institution will dictate cooperation. Thus cooperative social institutions emerge.

It is extremely important to note that, for the multilevel selection theory (or any other evolutionary theory, for that matter) to work, it makes absolutely no difference whether the process occurs genetically or culturally (Boyd and Richerson [1985]). What is necessary for evolution to occur is the *heritability of phenotypes:* Offspring must resemble their parents. The resemblance can happen because genes influence the phenotypes (such as cooperation or defection) or because the parents socialize their offspring to behave like them. Both processes work equally well for the evolution of cooperation. In fact, "parents" and "offspring" in the process of cultural evolution need not be genetically related at all. Cultural evolution works just as well when phenotypes are transmitted between unrelated individuals through teaching or imitation (Sober [1994]). One therefore need not assume that genes influence behavior at all, only that offspring (or students) resemble their parents (or teachers) and behave like them.

How Did the Unique Cooperative Institutions Emerge Only in Japan?

We now apply the general theory of the emergence of cooperative social institutions (derived from Sober and Wilson's multilevel selection theory) to explain why Japan has the unique institutions that foster dependence and visibility of group members. However, the particular forms that the institutions take are not as important as their effectiveness. Their particular forms (the mechanisms of dependence and visibility) can be quite accidental and result from historical path-dependence. What is important for us to explain instead is the fact that Japanese social institutions (whatever they are) seem to be most effective at inducing cooperation among groups and thereby producing group solidarity and thus social order. Why are Japanese social institutions more effective in producing group solidarity than institutions in other societies?

In order to answer this question, we begin with two observations. The first observation is that China is the only one of the six ancient civilizations (Mesopotamia, Egypt, the Indus Valley, North China, Mesoamerica, and Peru) that was never conquered and overtaken by foreign powers (until the Japanese occupation of Manchuria in the twentieth century). The other five ancient civilizations were eventually overrun by younger, European civilizations. When foreign powers invade and conquer a society, they usually introduce their own social institutions and supplant the native institutions. Thus, when Europeans invaded and colonized the five other civilizations, the native (old) institutions of these civilizations were largely replaced by the (younger) European institutions. China is the only ancient civilization where this supplanting of native institutions by foreign ones did not take place. China has kept its own social institutions. Since all the other societies of the world (and their social institutions) are by definition younger than the six ancient civilizations, it follows that China has the oldest surviving social institutions in the world.

The evolution of cooperation by multilevel selection occurs very slowly, as the proportion of cooperators in the population grows slowly generation after generation. It therefore takes a long time for cooperation, and thus cooperative social institutions, to emerge. Because the evolution of cooperation and cooperative institution takes a long time, it follows that older societies, on average, should have more cooperative social institutions than younger societies do or that older social institutions are, on average, more cooperative than younger ones. Although the multilevel selection theory predicts that the level of cooperation can sometimes reach an equilibrium, ceteris paribus, older institutions (which have had more time to evolve) are expected to be more cooperative than younger institutions (which have had less time to evolve).

Then the question is: Why Japan, not China? In order to answer this question, we make another observation. Many elements of culture in East Asia, from religion to the written language to the system of law and government, appear to have originated in China and were then transmitted to Korea and then finally to Japan (Fairbank, Reischauer, and Craig [1973]). Many cultural elements that can be observed in Japan today were borrowed from China through Korea. There is no reason to believe that cooperative social institutions are an exception to this rule.

Assume that cooperation and, along with it, cooperative social institutions, began to evolve in China sometime in the early history. Through the process of multilevel selection described in the previous section, cooperation evolved in China and Chinese groups become more and more cooperative. As we argue above, this happens because more cooperative groups grow faster than less cooperative groups. Because they are more adaptive and have higher solidarities, more cooperative groups thrive at the cost of less cooperative groups, and in the process replace them and their less cooperative social institutions. In the process of multilevel selection by which cooperation evolves, more cooperative groups are more ascendant and dominant than less cooperative groups.

If some groups in China were then to influence Korea, it is reasonable to assume that it is the more ascendant groups in the process of taking over the society, rather than the less ascendant ones in the process of being eliminated, that are more likely to influence other societies. So we suspect that more cooperative groups in China influenced Korea (because they were simultaneously more ascendant and dominant groups), and transmitted their cooperative social institutions to the Koreans. That means that, to the extent that this process of cultural transmission was uniform and widespread, the social institutions that the Koreans inherited from the Chinese were more cooperative than the average social institutions in China, because some groups in the latter, still in the process of being replaced, had less cooperative social institutions. As with other cultural elements imported from China, such as religion and the written language, we expect that the Chinese social institutions completely took over native Korean institutions and supplanted them.

The same process of multilevel selection could begin in Korea as soon as the institutions were inherited from China, as the same institutions continued to evolve in China. Eventually, given time, social institutions in both China and Korea will attain the maximum (or the equilibrium) level of cooperativeness. However, *at any given point in history, Korean social institutions should be slightly more cooperative than their counterparts in China*, because of the head start they had at the time of the cultural transmission. These social institutions were later transmitted from Korea to Japan by the ascendant and dominant groups in Korea. Then, by the same token, *Japanese social institutions should be slightly more cooperative than Korean social institutions at any given point in history*.

We do not expect the head start that Korea enjoyed over China and that Japan enjoyed over Korea to be large, and the evidence seems to indicate that both China and Korea have high levels of group solidarity and social order similar to (but not quite as high as) Japan (Hechter and Kanazawa [1993, tab. 1]). However, as long as it is always the ascendant and dominant groups that influence other societies, and the social institutions imported from a neighboring nation completely supplant the native ones (in the early history of East Asia), then the small head start enjoyed by nations later in the chain of cultural influence should foster more cooperative social institutions in these societies.

We speculate that this might be why Japanese social institutions are more cooperative than those found elsewhere in the world. First, China is the only ancient civilization that was not conquered by younger, European civilizations, and thus it retained its ancient, highly cooperative social institutions. Second, the unique history of cultural transmission from China to Korea then to Japan makes it likely that cooperative social institutions that Japan inherited from Korea are more effective than the ones that Korea inherited from China, which in turn are more effective than the ones evolving in China.

Conclusion

In this chapter, we first presented a general theory of the emergence of cooperative social institutions by drawing on the new theory of multilevel selection (Sober and Wilson [1998]). We then explained why Japan might have some of the most cooperative social institutions in the world. We emphasize that our ideas in this chapter are far more speculative than those presented in earlier chapters. Our theory of institutional emergence is new and has not been tested empirically (except in Kanazawa and Still [1999]), and our account of why Japan is unique in the strength of its cooperative social institutions is largely speculative.

11

Conclusion

Past studies of social order have tended to either focus on informal social control mechanisms in terms of internalized social norms and values, or formal social control in terms of the effectiveness of laws, police, and the criminal justice system. The focus of this book differed significantly from all of those studies. Although we acknowledge the importance of both internalized social norms and the criminal justice system, our focus has been on the role of small-group interactions and the production of social order. Since, unlike the socialization process and the criminal justice system, small-group interactions do not have the explicit purpose of promoting overall social order, we have referred to social order as an unintended consequence.

In searching for what is unique about Japanese society, several researchers have argued persuasively that it is not culture, per se, but rather the web of personal relationships and networks that exist at virtually all levels of society that is unique (Murakami and Rohlen [1992]; Kumon [1992]). These networks consist of both the tight-knit small groups that people belong to, and the loose-knit connections that exist between these groups. Past studies that have focused on the loose-knit connections, especially those involving the informal links between private organizations, government agencies, and financial institutions, were interested primarily in macro social structures and their effects on political and economic outcomes. Studies that focused on small-group interactions were typically limited in scope to explaining specific areas of society such as school life or work life. However, we have joined these two areas by showing how small-group interactions have macro-level consequences. Since the structure of group life creates an atmosphere where normative obligations are high and inappropriate behavior is quickly sanctioned, social order is produced and maintained. In other words, social order is not primarily maintained through the enactment of laws, the presence of police, or the actions of politicians or even religious leaders, as is the case in many countries. Rather, it is a by-product of a web of social networks and small groups, each maintaining order in pursuit of its own long-term objectives.

It is difficult to open a book on Japan that does not emphasize how it is uniquely "group-oriented." Unfortunately, the majority of these books then go on to misinterpret what is meant by "group-oriented." Rather than recognizing that participation in groups is necessary for achieving personal goals, they attribute this behavior to cultural values such as the desire for social harmony or social solidarity. Although these might, indeed, be cultural values (as they are in many societies), empirical studies have failed to uncover anything unique about Japan in this regard (see Mouer and Sugimoto [1986]). Thus there seems to be a fundamental misunderstanding of why it is that Japanese people participate in groups. A good example of this type of misunderstanding comes from discussions of the Japanese term *giri*, typically translated as "a sense of obligation." This is often associated with the Japanese "group-oriented" value system that places obligation to others above self-interests. Yet this is a misunderstanding of the term. As Mouer and Sugimoto (1986) point out, *giri* is more similar to a contractual relationship than a moral imperative. It is based on the concept of a reciprocal social exchange, where the person displaying a sense of obligation expects to benefit in the long run from that behavior.

Furthermore, as Yamagishi and his colleagues have demonstrated, once Japanese are removed from a structural environment that promotes group-oriented behavior, Japanese do not prefer groups. Indeed, it is interesting to note that when Japanese have free time, they typically prefer solitary activities such as watching television, reading, photography, going to movies, or playing pachinko. Preferences in sports tend to lean to more individualistic activities as well (e.g., golf, swimming, and distance running, as well as traditional Japanese martial arts). This has led a variety of researchers to reject the "group-oriented" model of Japanese society. But such a rejection is, we believe, also mistaken. Understanding the importance of small-group affiliations is the key to understanding much of modern Japanese society. What is necessary is to discard nebulous cultural explanations and concentrate on understanding the actual conditions under which most people in modern Japanese society now live.

We organized this book into four sections. The first section presented our theoretical perspective. This perspective is quite unique for studies of social order and also for studies of Japanese society in that it focuses exclusively on small-group interactions. The model we developed from this perspective was relatively simple, focusing primarily on just a few basic concepts such as group dependence and visibility. Nevertheless, it proved useful for understanding a great deal about modern Japanese society. Without invoking broad, nonspecific terms such as culture, ideology, and values, we were able to explain how social order in Japan is created and maintained, as well as a wide range of other macro-level social characteristics.

The second section followed the individual as he or she is introduced into Japanese society, and more specifically, into a variety of small-group settings. In each setting, beginning in preschool or kindergarten and moving through higher levels of education and then on to work and family life, the individual navigates through a network of relationships consisting of long-term reciprocal exchanges. The benefits of these relationships are considerable and range from long-term security to a dependable source of social and emotional support as well as material success. The price one pays for entry into these relationships is also considerable and includes a willingness to conform to a rigid set of normative obligations and also a willingness to defer receipt of those benefits to some later time.

The third section of this book sought to go beyond describing typical patterns of social life in Japan to exploring some of the nonintuitive consequences of this type of social structure. There are, no doubt, many such consequences (both positive and negative) but we chose to focus on three: white-collar crime, religion, and trust.

Virtually everyone familiar with Japan is aware of the country's low crime rates. A number of researchers have also noted the prevalence of white-collar crimes. However, it is not generally understood that the same social structural conditions responsible for one are also responsible for the other. Although intense small-group interactions and pressure to conform to conventional behavioral norms might attenuate certain types of street crimes, it appears to actually foster other types of crimes. Since white-collar crimes are often committed to increase the profits of one's company or to help important clients or colleagues, strong group loyalty and commitment might actually foster these types of crimes. In such cases, the same model that predicts behavioral conformity and high social order also predicts white-collar crime. To the degree that a person is dependent on the group and that the group participates in illegal activities, one would expect pressure to both participate in crimes and protect the group when those activities are uncovered.

Even less intuitive is the relationship between social structure and religion. Although Japan stands out among modern industrialized countries in terms of low crime rates, it also stands out in terms of the relative unimportance of organized religions. It would appear that these two characteristics are unrelated, but that is not the case. Both appear to be consequences of producing and maintaining social order through primary group affiliations and closed social networks. Not only does this structure reduce street crimes and increase white-collar crimes, but it also obviates the need for religious organizational affiliations. The Japanesee social structure reduces the need for religious affiliation in two ways. First, by encouraging strong group affiliations, the need for social and emotional support from other sources, such as religious organizations, is unnecessary. Second, secular group affiliations in Japan consume all of a person's free time, so there is no time to participate in other organizations. This does not mean that religion is unimportant in Japan, merely that membership-based organizations are not necessary. Secular affiliations, particularly work group affiliations, leave no room for additional loyalties. As Lincoln and Kalleberg (1990) state, Japanese companies are commitment-maximizing organizations.

Finally, recent research has uncovered another aspect of modern Japanese society that, on the surface, is puzzling. Japanese consistently exhibit low levels of "generalized trust," that is, trust in the benign intentions of others. As Yamagishi and his colleagues have pointed out, generalized trust is important in terms of freeing people from an overreliance on established relations, so that they can pursue better opportunities elsewhere. Once again, Japan's low level of generalized trust appears to be related to the same social structural conditions that affect crime rates and religious behavior. Because of the heavy reliance on group affiliation in Japan and the ability of the group to monitor and sanction inappropriate behavior, Japanese people live in a highly secure environment where others cannot cheat or take advantage of them. Because there is this "assurance" that one will not be cheated, there is no need to "trust" others (in the sense that trust entails putting oneself in a vulnerable position where others might take advantage of one). Thus, another unintended consequence of the Japanese style of producing and maintaining social order is the creation of a society characterized by low levels of generalized trust. This, in turn, could have important consequences in areas of international relations and business practices, where generalized trust is often an asset.

Finally, in Part Four we speculated as to why Japan developed the unique types of social institutions that it did. We did this by first developing a theory of the emergence of cooperative social institutions. Then we considered the unique historical situation by which ancient Chinese social institutions were introduced into Japanese society. The fact that these institutions have been preserved better in Japan than in China itself comes as no surprise. First, as we speculated in Chapter 10, it is likely that only the most evolved social institutions (i.e., the most cooperative) were transmitted to Japan in the first place. And second, Japan has had a very stable and isolated history, and many cultural elements originally imported from China, such as wearing kimonos and using tatami mats, have been well preserved despite the fact that they have long since disappeared from China.

We began this book by noting an ironic relationship between crime rates and Nobel Prize winners. Japan is exceptionally low in both categories, whereas the United States is exceptionally high. At that time, we noted that underlying this unusual statistic was the concept of social order. The Japanese social structure rewards conformity and punishes nonconformity. Therefore, Japanese society has achieved a very high level of social order. Unfortunately, criminals are not the only nonconformists in a society. Geniuses are also nonconformists. The United States, with its emphasis on individual freedom, has created a society with a relatively low degree of social order. Unfortunately, a society that affords its citizen free rein is unable to control where that freedom will lead. Americans are free to make scientific discoveries, and are also free to hold up a liquor store.

In the classic work *Leviathan*, seventeenth-century English philosopher Thomas Hobbes notes that life in its natural state is "solitary, poor, nasty, brutish, and short." In order to avoid this, he continues, humans developed societies where people voluntarily relinquished some of their personal freedoms in return for a safe and secure living environment. Thus, social order arose. However, the degree to which social order exists differs greatly from society to society, and finding the proper balance between order and personal freedom is no simple task. The authors of this book are, perhaps, a good example of the complexity of the situation. Both of us have spent a great deal of time living in both Japan and the United States, the two countries that arguably exhibit the two extremes in this area. One of us has chosen to live in Japan, finding the orderliness and safety well worth sacrifices in personal freedom. The other prefers to live in the United States, finding the Japanese social structure too confining and oppressive.

There appears, then, to be no clear answer to the questions posed at the outset of this book. How much social order is appropriate? How much is too much? Even the authors cannot agree on answers to these questions. Moreover, there is precious little here in terms of "lessons" for other societies. In reality, most Americans are happy living in America and do not want to live anywhere else. Most Japanese feel the same way about their country. Furthermore, if Americans were asked if they were willing to sacrifice a great deal of their personal freedom in order to increase their safety and security, they would likely answer no. Similarly, if Japanese were asked if they would like to increase their personal freedom, but the result would be a decrease in social order, they too would likely answer no. Perhaps it is best, then, not to try and resolve this issue, but instead to appreciate the variety of social systems that exist in the world, and be thankful to live in an international era where choice of one's home country is possible.

References

Abegglen, James C., and George Stalk, Jr. 1985. *Kaisha: The Japanese Corporation*. New York: Basic Books.

Abell, Ellen, and Viktor Gecas. 1997. "Guilt, Shame, and Family Socialization: A Retrospective Study." *Journal of Family Issues* 18:99.

Akers, Ronald L. 1985. *Deviant Behavior: A Social Learning Approach*. Belmont, Calif.: Woodsworth.

Akers, Ronald L., Marvin D. Krohn, Lonn Lanza-Kaduce, and Marcia Radosevich. 1979. "Social Learning and Deviant Behavior: A Specific Test of a General Theory." *American Sociological Review* 44:636–655.

Alletzhauser, Albert J. 1990. *The House of Nomura: The Inside Story of the Legendary Japanese Financial Dynasty*. New York: Arcade.

Amato, Paul R. 1993. "Children's Adjustment to Divorce: Theories, Hypotheses, and Empirical Support." *Journal of Marriage and the Family* 55:23–38.

Anesaki, Masaharu. 1930. *History of Japanese Religion*. London: Kegan Paul, Trench, Trubner and Co.

Bailey, William, J. David Martin, and Louis Gray. 1974. "Crime and Deterrence: A Correlational Analysis." *Journal of Research in Crime and Delinquency* 11:124–143.

Baker, Wayne. 1984. "The Social Structure of a National Securities Market." *American Journal of Sociology* 89:775–811.

Banfield, Edward. 1968. *The Unheavenly City*. Boston: Little, Brown, and Company.

Bayley, David H. 1991. *Forces of Order: Policing Modern Japan*, 2d ed. Berkeley: University of California Press.

Ben-Ari, Eyal, Brian Moeran, and James Valentine (eds.). 1990. *Unwrapping Japan: Society and Culture in Anthropological Perspective*. Honolulu: University of Hawaii Press.

Benedict, Ruth. 1946. *The Chrysanthemum and the Sword: Patterns of Japanese Culture*. Cambridge: Houghton Mifflin.

Binmore, Ken. 1994. *Game Theory and the Social Contract*, vol. 1 of *Playing Fair*. Cambridge: MIT Press.

_____. 1998. *Game Theory and the Social Contract*, vol. 2 of *Just Playing*. Cambridge: MIT Press.

Boyd, Robert, and Peter J. Richerson. 1985. *Culture and the Evolutionary Process*. Chicago: University of Chicago Press.

Braithwaite, John. 1989. *Crime, Shame and Reintegration*. Cambridge: Cambridge University Press.

Brinton, Mary. 1989. "Gender Stratification in Contemporary Urban Japan." *American Sociological Review* 54:542–557.

_____. 1993. *Women and the Economic Miracle: Gender and Work in Postwar Japan.* Berkeley: University of California Press.

Bronfenbrenner, Martin, and Yasukichi Yasuba. 1987. "Economic Welfare." Pp. 93–136 in *The Political Economy of Japan,* vol. 1, edited by Kozo Yamamura and Yasukichi Yasuba. Stanford: Stanford University Press.

Burgess, Robert L., and Ronald L. Akers. 1966. "A Differential Association-Reinforcement Theory of Criminal Behavior." *Social Problems* 14:128–147.

Bursik, Robert J. 1988. "Social Disorganization and Theories of Crime and Delinquency: Problems and Prospects." *Criminology* 26:519–551.

Cernkovich, Stephen A., and Peggy C. Giordano. 1992. "School Bonding, Race, and Delinquency." *Criminology* 30:261–291.

Chai, Sun-Ki, and Michael Hechter. 1998. "A Theory of the State and of Social Order." Pp. 33–60 in *The Problem of Solidarity,* edited by Thomas J. Fararo and Patrick Doreian. New York: Gordon and Breach.

Clark, Rodney C. 1979. *The Japanese Company.* New Haven, Conn: Yale University Press.

Clinard, Marshall B., and Richard Quinney. 1973. *Criminal Behavior Systems: A Typology.* New York: Holt, Rinehart, and Winston.

Clyde, Paul H., and Burton F. Beers. 1975. *The Far East: A History of Western Impacts and Eastern Responses, 1830–1975.* Englewood Cliffs, N.J.: Prentice-Hall.

Coleman, James W. 1985. *The Criminal Elite: The Sociology of White-Collar Crime.* New York: St. Martin's Press.

Committee for Comparative Survey of Value Systems. 1980. Tokyo: Marketing Service, Ltd.

Cook, Karen, and Richard Emerson. 1978. "Power, Equity and Commitment in Exchange Networks." *American Sociological Review* 43:721–739.

Cressey, Daniel R. 1960. "Epidemiology and Individual Conduct: A Case from Criminology." *Pacific Sociological Review* 3:47–58.

Davis, James A., and Tom W. Smith. 1996. *American General Social Survey, 1972–1996.* Chicago: NORC.

DiMaggio, Paul, and Hugh Louch. 1998. "Socially Embedded Consumer Transactions: For What Kinds of Purchases do People Most Often Use Networks?" *American Sociological Review* 63:619–637.

Doi, Takeo. 1973. *The Anatomy of Dependence.* Tokyo: Kodansha.

Dore, Ronald. 1987. *Taking Japan Seriously.* Stanford: Stanford University Press.

Dore, Ronald, Jean Bounine-Cabale, and Karl Topiola. 1989. *Japan at Work: Markets, Management and Flexibility.* Paris: OECD.

Earhart, H. Byron. 1970. *The New Religions of Japan.* Tokyo: Sophia University.

_____. 1982. *Japanese Religion: Unity and Diversity.* Belmont, Calif.: Wadsworth.

_____. 1984. *Religions of Japan: Many Traditions within One Sacred Way.* San Francisco: Harper and Row.

Elkin, Frederick, and Gerald Handel. 1978. *The Child and Society.* New York: Random House.

Ellickson, Robert C. 1991. *Order Without Law: How Neighbors Settle Disputes.* Cambridge: Harvard University Press.

Elster, Jon. 1989. *The Cement of Society: A Study of Social Order.* Cambridge: Cambridge University Press.

Fairbank, John K., Edwin O. Reischauer, and Albert M. Craig. 1973. *East Asia: Tradition and Transformation.* Boston: Houghton Mifflin.

Fallows, James. 1989. *More Like Us: Making America Great Again.* Boston: Houghton Mifflin.

Fishman, Gideon, and Simon Dinitz. 1989. "Japan: A Country with Safe Streets." Pp. 111–126 in William S. Laufer and Freda Adler (eds.), *Advances in Criminological Theory,* vol. 1. New Brunswick: Transaction.

Frohlich, Norman and Joe A. Oppenheimer. 1970. "I Get By With a Little Help From My Friends." *World Politics* 23:104–120.

Fujita, Hidenori. 1985. "The Structure of Opportunities for Status Attainment: The Role of Education and Social Tracking." *Research in Higher Education: Daigaku Ronshu* No. 14. Hiroshima: Hiroshima University Press.

Fukuyama, Francis. 1995. *Trust: The Social Virtues and Creation of Prosperity.* New York: Free Press.

Gibbs, Jack P. 1975. *Crime, Punishment, and Deterrence.* New York: Elsevier.

Glaser, Daniel. 1956. "Criminality Theories and Behavioral Images." *American Journal of Sociology* 61:433–444.

Glock, Charles, Benjamin Ringer, and Earl Babbie. 1967. *To Comfort and to Challenge.* Berkeley: University of California Press.

Goode, Erich. 1990. *Deviant Behavior.* Englewood Cliffs, N.J.: Prentice-Hall.

Gordon, Andrew. 1985. *The Evolution of Labor Relations in Japan: Heavy Industry 1853–1955.* Cambridge: Harvard University Press.

Grant, Don Sherman, and Ramiro Martinez. 1997. "Crime and the Restructuring of the U.S. Economy: A Reconsideration of Class Linkages." *Social Forces* 75:769–797.

Gray, Louis N., and J. David Martin. 1969. "Punishment and Deterrence: Another Analysis." *Social Science Quarterly* 50:389–395.

Groves, W. Byron, and Nancy Frank. 1987. "Punishment, Privilege and the Sociology of Structured Choice." In W. Byron Groves and Graeme Newman (eds.), *Punishment and Privilege.* Albany, N.Y.: Harrow and Heston.

Hagan, John. 1994. *Crime and Disrepute.* Thousand Oaks, Calif.: Pine Forge Press.

Haley, John O. 1986. "Comment: The Implications of Apology." *Law and Society Review* 20:499–507.

Hamilton, V. Lee, and Joseph Sanders. 1996. "Corporate Crime Through Citizens' Eyes: Stratification and Responsibility in the United States, Russia, and Japan." *Law and Society Review* 30:513–547.

Hampton, Jean. 1986. *Hobbes and the Social Contract Tradition.* Cambridge: Cambridge University Press.

Hardacre, Helen. 1984. *Lay Buddhism in Contemporary Japan.* New Jersey: Princeton University Press.

_____. 1986. *Kurozumikyo and the New Religions of Japan.* Princeton, N.J.: Princeton University Press.

Harris, Marvin. 1980. *Cultural Materialism: The Struggle for a Science of Culture.* New York: Vintage.

Hayashi, Chikio, Hiroshi Akuto, and Fumi Hayashi. 1977. *A Survey of Customs and Traditions*. Tokyo: Institute of Statistical Mathematics.

Hayashi, Chikio, Tatsuzo Suzuki, Giichiro Suzuki, and Masakatsu Murakami. 1982. *A Study of Japanese National Character*, Vol. 4. Tokyo: Idemitsushoten.

Hechter, Michael. 1987. *Principles of Group Solidarity*. Berkeley: University of California Press.

_____. 1989. "Rational Choice Foundations of Social Order." Pp. 60–81 in *Theory Building in Sociology: Assessing Theoretical Cumulation*, edited by Jonathan H. Turner. Newbury Park, Calif.: Sage Publications.

_____. 1990. "The Emergence of Cooperative Social Institutions." Pp. 13–33 in *Social Institutions: Their Emergence, Maintenance, and Effects*, edited by Michael Hechter, Karl-Dieter Opp, and Reinhard Wippler. New York: Aldine.

_____. 1993. "From Group Solidarity to Social Order." Paper presented at the Workshop on Law, Economics and Organization, Yale Law School, November 4.

Hechter, Michael, Debra Friedman, and Satoshi Kanazawa. 1992. "The Attainment of Global Order in Heterogeneous Societies." Pp. 79–97 in *Rational Choice Theory: Advocacy and Critique*, edited by James S. Coleman and Thomas J. Fararo. Newbury Park, Calif.: Sage.

Hechter, Michael, and Satoshi Kanazawa. 1993. "Group Solidarity and Social Order in Japan." *Journal of Theoretical Politics* 5:455–493.

Hendry, Joy. 1986. "Kindergartens and the Transition from Home to School Education." *Comparative Education* 22:53–58.

_____. 1993. *Wrapping Culture: Politeness, Presentation, and Power in Japan and Other Societies*. Oxford: Clarendon.

Hirschi, Travis. 1969. *Causes of Delinquency*. Berkeley: University of California Press.

_____. 1995. *Causes of Delinquency: Seeking the Interconnection Among Family, School and Society* (Hiko no Gen'in: Katei Gakko Shakai no Tsunagari wo Motomete). Translated by Yoji Morita and Shinji Shimizu. Tokyo: Bunka Shobo.

Holtom, D. C. 1963. *Modern Japan and Shinto Nationalism*. New York: Paragon Books.

Homans, George C. 1950. *The Human Group*. New York: Harcourt Brace and World.

Hori, Ichiro, Ikado Fujio, Wakimoto Tsuneya, and Yanagawa Keiishi (eds.). 1972. *Japanese Religion: A Survey by the Agency of Cultural Affairs*. Tokyo: Kodansha.

Imada, Takatoshi, and Junsuke Hara. 1979. "Shakaitekichi no Ikkansei to Hikkansen" (Status Consistency and Inconsistency). Pp. 161–197 in *Nihon no Kaiso Kozo* (Social Stratification in Japan), edited by Ken'ichi Tominaga. Tokyo: University of Tokyo Press.

Ishida, Takeshi. 1971. *Japanese Society*. New York: Random House.

Iwao, Sumiko. 1995. "The Quiet Revolution: Japanese Women Today." Pp. 180–193 in *Comparing Cultures*, edited by Merri I. White and Sylvan Barnet. Boston: Bedford Books.

Iwata, Ryushi. 1992. "The Japanese Enterprise as a Unified Body of Employees: Origins and Developments." Pp. 170–197 in *The Political Economy of Japan*, vol. 3, edited by Shumpei Kumon and Henry Rosovsky. Stanford: Stanford University Press.

Japan Almanac. 1998. Asahi Shimbun Publishing Company.

Japan External Trade Organization (Jetro). 1991. *U.S. and Japan in Figures* (Nihon to Amerika: Suji wa Kataru). Tokyo: Japan External Trade Organization.

Kamo, Yoshinori. 1990. "Husbands and Wives Living in Nuclear and Stem Family Households in Japan." *Sociological Perspectives* 33:397–417.

Kanazawa, Satoshi. 1997. "A Solidaristic Theory of Social Order." Pp. 81–111 in *Advances in Group Processes*, vol. 14, edited by Barry Markovsky, Michael Lovaglia, and Lisa Troyer. Greenwich, Conn.: JAI Press.

Kanazawa, Satoshi, and Debra Friedman. 1999. "The State's Contribution to Social Order in National Societies: Somalia as an Illustrative Case." *Journal of Political and Military Sociology* 27 (1): 1–20.

Kanazawa, Satoshi, and Mary C. Still. 1999. "Why Monogamy?" *Social Forces* 78: 25–50.

Kerbo, Harold R., and Mariko Inoue. 1990. "Japanese Social Structure and White Collar Crime: Recruit Cosmos and Beyond." *Deviant Behavior* 11:139–154.

Kida, Hiroshi. 1986. "Educational Administration in Japan." *Comparative Education* 22:7–12.

Kikuchi, Masako, Yoriko Watanabe, and Toshio Yamagishi. 1997. "Judgment Accuracy of Other's Trustworthiness and General Trust: An Experimental Study" (Tasha no Shinraisei Handan no Seikakusa to Ippanteki Shinrai—Jikken Kenkyu). *Japanese Journal of Experimental Social Psychology* (Jikken Shakai Shinrigaku Kenkyu) 37:23–36.

Kitagawa, Joseph M. 1987. *On Understanding Japanese Religion.* Princeton, N.J.: Princeton University Press.

Kiyonari, Tohko, and Toshio Yamagishi. 1996. "Distrusting Outsiders as a Consequence of Commitment Formation" (Komitomento Keisei ni yoru Bugaisha ni Taisuru Shinrai no Teika). *Japanese Journal of Experimental Social Psychology* (Jikken Shakai Shinrigaku Kenkyu) 36:56–67.

Knight, Jack. 1992. *Institutions and Social Conflict.* Cambridge: Cambridge University Press.

Kodera, Kyoko. 1994. "The Reality of Equality for Japanese Female Workers: Women's Careers Within the Japanese Style of Management." *Social Justice* 21:136–154.

Kollock, Peter. 1993a. "'An Eye for an Eye Leaves Everyone Blind': Cooperation and Accounting Systems." *American Sociological Review* 58:768–786.

_____. 1993b. "Cooperation in an Uncertain World: An Experimental Study." *Sociological Theory and Methods* 8:3–18.

_____. 1994. "The Emergence of Exchange Structures: An Experimental Study of Uncertainty, Commitment, and Trust." *American Journal of Sociology* 100:313–345.

_____. 1998. "Social Dilemmas: The Anatomy of Cooperation." *Annual Review of Sociology* 24:183–214.

Kornhauser, Ruth. 1978. *Social Sources of Delinquency: An Appraisal of Analytic Models.* Chicago: University of Chicago Press.

Kumon, Shumpei. 1992. "Japan as a Network Society." Pp. 109–141 in *The Political Economy of Japan*, vol. 3, edited by Shumpei Kumon and Henry Rosovsky. Stanford: Stanford University Press.

Laub, John H. 1983. "Urbanism, Race, and Crime." *Journal of Research on Crime and Delinquency* 20:183–198.

Lebra, Takie Sugiyama. 1976. *Japanese Patterns of Behavior.* Honolulu: University of Hawaii Press.

Lewis, Catherine C. 1984. "Cooperation and Control in Japanese Nursery Schools." *Comparative Education Review* 28:69–84.

_____. 1988. "Japanese First-Grade Classrooms: Implications for U.S. Theory and Research." *Comparative Education Review* 32:159–172.

_____. 1989. "From Indulgence to Internalization: Social Control in the Early School Years." *Journal of Japanese Studies* 15:139–157.

Lincoln, James R., and Arne L. Kalleberg. 1990. *Culture, Control and Commitment: A Study of Work Organization and Work Attitudes in the United States and Japan.* Cambridge: Cambridge University Press.

Liska, Allen E. 1987. *Perspectives on Deviance.* Englewood Cliffs, N.J.: Prentice-Hall.

Lofland, John, and Rodney Stark. 1965. "Becoming a World-Saver: A Theory of Conversion to a Deviant Perspective." *American Sociological Review* 30:862–75.

Long, Susan Orpett. 1987. *Family Change and the Life Course in Japan.* Ithaca, N.Y.: Cornell University Press.

Macy, Michael W. 1989. "Walking Out of Social Traps: A Stochastic Learning Model for Prisoner's Dilemma." *Rationality and Society* 1:197–219.

_____. 1990. "Learning Theory and the Logic of Critical Mass." *American Sociological Review* 55:809–826.

_____. 1991a. "Learning to Cooperate: Stochastic and Tacit Collusion in Social Exchange." *American Journal of Sociology* 97:808–843.

_____. 1991b. "Chains of Cooperation: Threshold Effects in Collective Action." *American Sociological Review* 56:730–747.

Maguire, Kathleen, Ann L. Pastore, and Timothy J. Flanagan, eds. 1993. *Sourcebook of Criminal Justice Statistics.* U.S. Department of Justice, Bureau of Justice Statistics. Washington, D.C.: U.S. Government Printing Office.

Maraini, Fosco. 1975. "Japan and the Future: Some Suggestions from Nihonjinron Literature." Pp. 17–19 in *Social Structures and Economic Dynamics in Japan up to 1980,* edited by Gianni Fodella. Milan: Institute of Economic and Social Studies for East Asia.

Matsueda, Ross L., and Karen Heimer. 1987. "Race, Family Structure, and Delinquency: A Test of Differential Association and Social Control Theories." *American Sociological Review* 52:826–840.

McCaghy, Charles H., and Timothy A. Capron. 1997. *Deviant Behavior: Crime, Conflict, and Interest Groups.* Needham Heights, Mass.: Allyn and Bacon.

McCandless, Boyd R. 1969. "Childhood Socialization." In *Handbook of Socialization Theory and Research,* edited by D. A. Goslin. Chicago: Rand McNally.

McFarland, H. Neill. 1970. *The Rush Hour of the Gods.* New York: Harper and Row.

Miller, Alan S. 1991. "Testing a Model of Religiosity in a Non-Western Setting: An Evaluation of Religiosity in Japan." Ph.D. dissertation. University of Washington, Department of Sociology.

_____. 1992a. "Conventional Religious Behavior in Modern Japan: A Service Industry Perspective. *Journal for the Scientific Study of Religion* 31:207–214.

_____. 1992b. "Predicting Nonconventional Religious Affiliation in Tokyo: A Control Theory Application." *Social Forces* 71:397–410.

_____. 1995. "A Rational Choice Model for Religious Behavior in Japan." *Journal for the Scientific Study of Religion* 34:234–244.

_____. 1998. "Why Japanese Religions Look Different: The Social Role of Religious Organizations in Japan." *Review of Religious Research* 39:379–389.

Miller, Alan S., and John P. Hoffmann. 1995. "Risk and Religion: An Explanation of Gender Differences in Religiosity." *Journal for the Scientific Study of Religion* 34:63–75.

Monbusho. 1998. "White Paper on Educational Reform. Ministry of Education, Science, Sports and Culture." URL: www.monbu.go.jp.

Morioka, Kiyomi. 1975a. *Religion in Changing Japanese Society*. Tokyo: University of Tokyo Press.

_____. 1975b. *Modern Society's People and Religion: Japanese Behavior and Thought* (Gendai Shakai no Minshu to Shukkyo). Tokyo: Hyoronsha.

Mouer, Ross, and Yoshio Sugimoto. 1986. *Images of Japanese Society*. London: Routledge and Kegan Paul.

Murakami, Shigeyoshi. 1968. *Japanese Religion in the Modern Century*. Translated by H. Byron Earhart. Tokyo: University of Tokyo Press.

Murakami, Yasusuke. 1978. "The Reality of the New Middle Class." *Japan Interpreter* 12:1–5.

Murakami, Yasusuke, Shumpei Kumon, and Seizaburo Sato. 1979. Bunmei to Shite no Ie Shakai (Ie Society as a Pattern of Civilization). Tokyo: Chuokoronsha.

Murakami, Yasusuke, and Thomas P. Rohlen. 1992. "Social Exchange Aspects of the Japanese Political Economy: Culture, Efficiency, and Change." Pp. 63–105 in *The Political Economy of Japan*, vol. 3, edited by Shumpei Kumon and Henry Rosovsky. Stanford: Stanford University Press.

Mussen, Paul H., John J. Conger, and Jerome Kagan. 1974. Child Development and Personality. New York: Harper and Row.

Nakane, Chie. 1970. *Japanese Society*. Berkeley: University of California Press.

National Center for Educational Statistics. 1996. *National Educational Longitudinal Study: 1988–94*. Washington, D.C.: U.S. Department of Education.

Nishio, Kanji. 1985. *Japanese Education: Wisdom and Contradiction* (Nihon no Kyoiku: Chie to Mujun). Tokyo: Chuokoronsha.

Nishiyama, Tadanori, and Koji Matsumoto. 1983. *The Rise of Corporatism: The Hero of Japanese Power* (Kigyo-shugi no Koryu: Nihon-teki Pawa no Shuyaku). Tokyo: Nihon Seisansei Honbu.

Numata, Kenya. 1995. *Neo-Paradigm in Religion and Science: A Discussion of the New New Religions* (Shukkyo to Kagaku no Neoparadaimu: Shinshin Shukkyo wo Chushin to Shite). Tokyo: Sogensha.

Ojima, Fumiaki, Toru Kikkawa, Makoto Todoroki, Souhei Aramaki, Yasunori Kudo, and Asako Kotani. 1998. "Research on the Change in Career Plans of High School Seniors; A Replicated Survey in 1981 and 1997" (Gendai Kokosei no Shinro to Seikatsu: Sono Kozo to Henyo). *Research Report of Grant-in-Aid Scientific Research*. Osaka: Osaka University of Economics.

Ojima, Fumiaki, and Alan S. Miller. 1992. "Lifestyle Differentiation and Social Stratification" (Raifusutairu no Bunka to Shakaikaiso). *Journal of Osaka University of Economics* (Osaka Keidai Ronshu) 43:119–139.

Okihara, Yutaka. 1986. "Educational Administration in Japan." *Comparative Education* 22:13–18.

Olson, Mancur. 1965. *The Logic of Collective Action: Public Goods and the Theory of Groups.* Cambridge: Harvard University Press.

Orbell, John, and Robyn M. Dawes. 1991. "A 'Cognitive Miser' Theory of Cooperators' Advantage." *American Political Science Review* 85:515–528.

_____. 1993. "Social Welfare, Cooperators' Advantage, and the Option of Not Playing the Game." *American Sociological Review* 58:787–800.

Ostrom, Elinor. 1990. *Governing the Commons: The Evolution of Institutions for Collective Action.* Cambridge: Cambridge University Press.

Ostrom, Elinor, James Walker, and Roy Gardner. 1992. "Covenants With and Without a Sword: Self-Enforcement Is Possible." *American Political Science Review* 86:404–417.

Park, Robert E., Ernest W. Burgess, and Roderick McKenzie. 1925. *The City.* Chicago: University of Chicago Press.

Parsons, Talcott. 1937. *The Structure of Social Action.* New York: McGraw Hill.

Patterson, Gerald R., and Thomas J. Dishion. 1985. "Contributions of Families and Peers to Delinquency." *Criminology* 23:63–79.

Peak, Lois. 1987. "Learning to Go to School in Japan: The Transition from Home to School Life." Ph.D. dissertation. Harvard University School of Education.

_____. 1989. "Learning to Become Part of the Group: The Japanese Child's Transition to Preschool Life." *Journal of Japanese Studies* 15:93–123.

Posner, Eric A. 1996. "The Regulation of Groups: The Influence of Legal and Nonlegal Sanctions on Collective Action." *University of Chicago Law Review* 63:133–197.

Reingold, Edwin M. 1995. "Common Crime, Common Criminals." Pp. 373–378 in *Comparing Cultures*, edited by Merri I. White and Sylvan Barnet. Boston: Bedford Books.

Reischauer, Edwin O. 1978. *The Japanese.* Cambridge: Harvard University Press.

Rohlen, Thomas P. 1974. *For Harmony and Strength: Japanese White-Collar Organization in Anthropological Perspective.* Berkeley: University of California Press.

_____. 1983. *Japan's High Schools.* Berkeley: University of California Press.

_____. 1989. "Order in Japanese Society: Attachment, Authority, and Routine." *Journal of Japanese Studies* 15:5–40.

_____. 1992. "Learning: The Mobilization of Knowledge in the Japanese Political Economy." Pp. 321–363 in *The Political Economy of Japan*, vol. 3, edited by Shumpei Kumon and Henry Rosovsky. Stanford: Stanford University Press.

Rosenbaum, James E., and Takehiko Kariya. 1989. "From High School to Work: Market and Institutional Mechanisms in Japan." *American Journal of Sociology* 94:1334–1365.

Sampson, Robert J. 1987. "Urban Black Violence: The Effects of Male Joblessness and Family Disruption." *American Journal of Sociology* 93:348–382.

_____. 1988. "Local Friendship Ties and Community Attachment in Mass Society: A Multilevel Systemic Model." *American Sociological Review* 53:766–779.

Sampson, Robert J., and W. Byron Groves. 1989. "Community Structure and Crime: Testing Social Disorganization Theory." *American Journal of Sociology* 94:774–802.

Sampson, Robert J., and John H. Laub. 1990. "Crime and Deviance over the Life Course: The Salience of Adult Social Bonds." *American Sociological Review* 55:609–627.

Sasaki, Masamichi, and Tatsuzo Suzuki. 1987. "Changes in Religious Commitment in the United States, Holland and Japan." *American Journal of Sociology* 92:1055–1076.

Schilling, Mark. 1994. *Sumo: A Fan's Guide*. Tokyo: *Japan Times*.

Schur, Edwin M. 1983. *Labeling Women Deviant: Gender, Stigma, and Social Control*. Philadelphia: Temple University Press.

Shaw, Clifford R., and Henry D. McKay. 1942. *Juvenile Delinquency and Urban Areas*. Chicago: University of Chicago Press.

Sherkat, Darren E., and John Wilson. 1995. "Preferences, Constraints, and Choice in Religious Markets: An Examination of Religious Switching and Apostasy." *Social Forces* 73:993–1026.

Shoham, S. Giora, and John P. Hoffmann. 1991. *A Primer in the Sociology of Crime*. Albany, N.Y.: Harrow and Heston.

Smith, Robert J. 1985. *Japanese Society: Tradition, Self and the Social Order*. Cambridge: Cambridge University Press.

Sober, Elliott. 1994. "Models of Cultural Evolution." Pp. 477–492 in *Conceptual Issues in Evolutionary Biology*, 2d ed. Cambridge: MIT Press.

Sober, Elliott, and David Sloan Wilson. 1998. *Unto Others: The Evolution and Psychology of Unselfish Behavior*. Cambridge: Cambridge University Press.

South, Scott J., and Steven F. Messner. 1987. "The Sex Ratio of Women's Involvement in Crime: A Cross-National Analysis." *Sociological Quarterly* 28:171–188.

Spiro, Melford E. 1966. "Religion and the Irrational." Pp. 102–115 in *Symposium on New Approaches to the Study of Religion*. Seattle: University of Washington Press.

Stark, Rodney. 1998. *Sociology*, 7th ed. Belmont, Calif.: Wadsworth.

Stark, Rodney, and William Sims Bainbridge. 1980. "Networks of Faith: Interpersonal Bonds and Recruitment to Cults and Sects." *American Journal of Sociology* 85:1376–1395.

_____. 1985. *The Future of Religions*. Berkeley: University of California Press.

_____. 1987. *A Theory of Religion*. New York: Peter Lang.

Steffensmeier, Darrell J., Emilie Anderson Allan, Miles D. Harer, and Cathy Streifel. 1989. "Age and the Distribution of Crime." *American Journal of Sociology* 94:803–831.

Sutherland, Edwin H. 1947. *Principles of Criminology*. Philadelphia: Lippincott.

Tasker, Peter. 1989. *The Japanese: A Portrait of a Nation*. New York: Meridian.

Taylor, Jared. 1983. *Shadows of the Rising Sun*. New York: Quill.

Triandis, Harry C. 1994. *Culture and Social Behavior*. New York: McGraw-Hill.

_____. 1995. *Individualism and Collectivism*. Boulder, Colo.: Westview Press.

Tsukahara, Shuuichi, Yoshiaki Noro, and Junichi Kobayashi. 1990. "Area and So-
cial Stratification" (Chiki to Shakaikaisou). Pp. 127–149 in *Social Stratification in Contemporary Japan*, vol. 1 (Gendai Nihon no Kaiso Kozo 1 Shakai Kaiso no Kozo to Katei), edited by Kazuo Seiyama and Atsushi Naoi. Tokyo: University of Tokyo Press.

Turnbull, Colin. 1983. *The Human Cycle*. New York: Simon and Schuster.

van Wolferen, Karel. 1989. *The Enigma of Japanese Power: People and Politics in a Stateless Nation*. New York: Knopf.

Vogel, Ezra F. 1985. *Japan as Number One: Lessons for America*. Cambridge: Harvard University Press.

Wallerstein, Judith, and Sandra Blakeslee. 1989. *Second Chances: Men, Women and Children a Decade after Divorce*. New York: Ticknor and Fields.

Watanabe, Kazuko. 1995. "The New Cold War with Japan: How are Women Pay-
ing for It?" Pp. 171–179 in *Comparing Cultures*, edited by Merry I. White and Sylvan Barnet. Boston: Bedford Books.

Weber, Max. 1968 [1922]. *Economy and Society*. Edited by Guenther Roth and Klaus Wittich. New York: Bedminster Press.

Wiatrowski, Michael D., David B. Griswold, and Mary K. Roberts. 1981. "Social Control Theory and Delinquency." *American Sociological Review* 46:525–541.

Willer, David, and Bo Anderson (eds.). 1981. *Networks, Exchange and Coercion: The Elementary Theory and Its Applications*. New York: Elsevier.

Wilson, Edward O. 1980. *Sociobiology*, abridged edition. Cambridge: Harvard University Press.

Wolfgang, Marvin E., and Franco Ferracuti. 1967. *The Subculture of Violence*. London: Travistock.

Woronoff, Jon. 1980. *Japan: The Coming Social Crisis*. Tokyo: Yohan Lotus Press.

_____. 1983. *Japan's Wasted Workers*. Totowa, N.J.: Allanheld, Osmun.

Wrong, Dennis H. 1994. *The Problem of Order: What Unites and Divides Society*. New York: Free Press.

Yamagishi, Toshio. 1988a. "Exit from the Group as an Individualistic Solution to the Free Rider Problem in the United States and Japan." *Journal of Experimental Social Psychology* 24:530–542.

_____. 1988b. "The Provision of a Sanctioning System in the United States and Japan." *Social Psychology Quarterly* 51:265–271.

_____. 1998. *The Structure of Trust* (Shinrai no Kozo). Tokyo: University of Tokyo Press.

Yamagishi, Toshio, Nobuhito Jin, and Alan S. Miller. 1998. "In-Group Bias and Culture of Collectivism." *Asian Journal of Social Psychology* 1:315–328.

Yamagishi, Toshio, and Midori Yamagishi. 1994. "Trust and Commitment in the United States and Japan." *Motivation and Emotion* 18:129–166.

Yamagishi, Toshio, Midori Yamagishi, Nobuyuki Takahashi, Nahoko Hayashi, and Motoki Watabe. 1995. "Trust and Commitment Formation: An Experimental Study" (Shinrai to Komitomento Keisei Jikken Kenkyu). *Japanese Journal of Experimental Social Psychology* (Jikken Shakai Shinrigaku Kenkyu) 35:23–34.

Yinger, Milton. 1970. *The Scientific Study of Religion*. London: Macmillan.

Yuki, Masaki. 1996. "Long-Term Equity Within a Group: An Application of the Seniority Norm in Japan." Pp. 288–297 in *Key Issues in Cross-Cultural Psychol-*

ogy: Selected Papers from the 12th International Congress of the International Association for Cross-Cultural Psychology, edited by Hector Grad, Amalio Blanco, and James Georgas. Lisse, Netherlands: Swets and Zeitlinger.

_____. 1998. "Transrelational Reciprocity as a Principle of Intergenerational Justice." Ph.D. dissertation. Tokyo University, Department of Social Psychology.

Index